Snapshots of a Curious Life

Ian Le Brunn

1. <u>To See A Man About a Dog</u>

The plough rocked and rolled in its nauseating rhythm along the furrows of an unrecognisable field. Beneath its share, the brown earth crumbled in crashing cymbals of sound. Insects scampered. Worms twisted and writhed. Flints and chalk ; flints and chalk.

What else was under the soil? Why did the boy endlessly dream about its churning and turning and crumbling?

The still and silent night was hot and dark now. The little boy roused himself and screwed up and blinked his eyes to unstick his zipped eyelids. His eyes opened to the dark brown of his room. He felt sick after the recurring dream of the field. His dizzy, sickening vantage point was just above the earth. Hovering.

'Night time', he murmured to himself. 'Still dark.' He rolled over onto the middle of the mattress and his unsettled body trembled.

Beside his bed in the small cot slept his sister. He could not see her in the brown room but nonetheless he could hear her gentle and relaxed breathing.

For some time now his dreams had brought him this unsettling sensation. The dreams always took him to a place where he was transfixed; pinned into place; only able to watch crumbling, cascading and sliding of ploughed earth. Like the other occasions he woke with its smell in his nostrils. He could hear it smashing down as the waves of earth rolled on over the plough share.

During these early years the recurrent ploughing dream dominated much of his sleeping time. When sleep came, the dream came. He was always alone. Alone and contending with the activity of the dream. When it was happening he could concentrate and focus with intensity- and still deal with the experience of rocking and the seasickness induced by the rhythm of the plough. There was never a ploughman. At least he never saw one. The boy never saw a person or a face. The plough seemed to travel forward of its own volition. Perhaps he was the ploughman.

His father was rarely there. The house was quiet. The nearby river was dark and dangerous; and if his father had been there, perhaps he could explain things. Dad never explained things. He just turned up in a random way as if he had never been away. Life was puzzling. Life was unpredictable. Yet somehow the boy knew he would come through the muddle. There were enough signs in his daily life for the boy to know he would come through the confusion. But it was a muddling through.

People came and went from the riverside cottage. One time a man smelling of oil came and lodged in the spare room. He collected insects and secured them in their display boxes with a pin through the abdomen. He brought earwigs which did battle with centipedes; and scorpions which menacingly held their angry little whips above their heads.

Another time a pair of twin brothers came. One had broken his ankle. On yet another occasion a photographer came and the boy, his younger sister, his mother and grandmother all stood outside the front of the cottage beneath the crumbling wall. He and his sister were photographed while mother and grandmother smiled.

Once, his father came home, with puppies. There were three young Alsatians, all bitches. His plan was to breed them. On another occasion his father came to the school to meet him. The boy never knew that his father would come. Nothing could be predicted. He had affection for his father but it was disconnected affection.

Their lives had brought them to the small village beside the ancient barn and the little church. The muddy banked river snaked around behind the house. Opposite the child's solitary cottage, a row of poor looking dwelling houses like a grey wall looked down on his room. The cottage was down in the dip and no getting away from it. But it was home.

The cottage represented the end of a long journey he and his mother, sister and father had travelled; from house to house, from tenement to tenement, from caravan to bus; from flat to cottage; any place to some place.

Moored alongside the cottage was his father's boat of dark and pale blue with its white trimmings. His father was handy with a boat. He had experience on rivers and knew something about diesel engines. The father was confident when he took his son out onto the river, despite the muddiness of its waters, and the unpredictability of this tidal stretch.

His father watched the river carefully; aware of the heavily laden barges with their cargoes of white foamy pulp plodding along to the paper mills at New Hythe. The skippers often tooted or waved especially if the village boys were swimming with their huge inflated inner tubes.

In the boat neither father nor son wore lifejackets but there were bright red and white safety rings, just in case something nasty happened. The little diesel engine signalled its readiness with its familiar 'phut..phut..phut' and cloud of bluish smoke.

On this occasion his father was keen to introduce the dogs to the water. Together, the three Alsatians were all led by his father to the water's edge and he then lifted his son onto the boat and stepped aboard himself. This action set the dogs into a frenzy of activity when they saw the master push the boat from the shore; scramble aboard with his son out into the river's eddies.

They barked and raced along the bank; they barked again, one quite hysterically; they rocked between land and water but it was only 'Judy' that jumped in and started paddling towards the boat.

'Come on girl...come on Judy' yelled the father, 'keep going girl; that's good; there's a good girl!'

After the father's encouragement, the dog worked harder and harder and slowly she neared the side of the boat. In an instant the father deftly scooped her from the water and soon she was wrapped in a handy towel and rubbed dry. The dog was his father's favourite. But the time the boy spent with his father was very short, especially when compared to Billy Antry across the road.

Billy's father lived there all the time and so he took his father for granted and rarely mentioned him. The boy always told his friend about his father's comings and goings; how he had been briefly in the army and was now in the merchant navy. But the boy never shared the story of his final meeting with his father before he left; he kept that to himself for years.

Alongside the boy, his sister snuffled in the brown night. A few spatters of rain splashed the window pane. The meeting with his Dad came into his mind. He saw the image of the school fence, running parallel with School Lane and his father being there and waiting for him as he came out.

'Hi son. Are you coming along? We're going to see Nana and Grandad.'

He remembered the train journey up to London. He recalled arriving at the terraced house where his grandparents lived. It smelled of cigarettes and Foxes glacier mints. They hugged him and swept him up because he was their 'dream boy', all they'd ever wanted in a grandson.

The night was spent on a white mattress with fine black stripes. His father climbed in beside him later in the night. They left the next day and all he could remember was the journey aboard the steam train and the question his father had asked him on their return.

Another gust rattled the old carriage window. The rain came across the river from the easterly direction of the sea. The boy snuggled down into the blanket but he was wide awake.

'Who do you want to be with,' asked his dad, 'your mum or with me?'

The boy looked out of the window. The steam from the engine drifted off across the fields of Kent. He didn't know what to say. He didn't want to say the wrong thing. He couldn't choose between his father and mother. It was too difficult. He hesitated.

 In his momentary thoughts he touched on the randomness of his father; the distance between them; and his mother's warmth and her continuous presence in his life.

He spoke quietly and clearly. 'I want to stay with my mum.' He paused and repeated his words in the hope they might come out differently.

'I want to stay with Mum. We'll all live in the cottage.'

'Alright' said his father. 'Alright' he repeated and he sighed. 'That's fine.' The boy being so young did not and could not read his father's face. He would never really know whether his answer was 'alright' and 'fine.'

After that journey his father never returned to the cottage. His Grandmother on his mother's side moved in to help her daughter.

The two women had come into England from Ireland in 1947, the grandmother leaving her daughter Maeve, his mother leaving her younger sister behind. Part of the reason for their flight from Ireland was of course an economic one, the search for work; the Irish condition. Jobs in Scrigg, County Mayo, where grandmother had lived with her husband; and also in her childhood home villages of Fordstown and Rathmolyon, were hard to come by.

When his Grandmother moved on to Dublin she again fell on hard times. Years later she told the boy about the treatment she had suffered at the hands of a Dublin family.

For months she worked for them, never missing a day through illness or an hour through lateness, until one day when her regular bus transport broke down and she was late to work. The family dismissed her on the spot. It was against the economic background coupled with some disillusion about her countrymen and women and her fear of her vindictive, brutal, pursuing husband that drove grandmother and daughter on their journey on the ferry.

Soon afterwards his mother had carelessly fallen out with the London family for whom she was a childminder and left the family to work at the local baker's shop. It was here she met his father and had quickly fallen pregnant with her first child.

To escape his predicament, his father stupidly joined the army in the February, taking off a couple of weeks for the birth of his son. A month later he had been discharged as 'unfit for military service.'

The couple had married at the registry office in June of 1950 and the boy was born in the October of that year. Without his father, the cottage felt different for the boy. He was conscious of being the only male around the house, even though he was called 'the young fella' by his grandmother and 'young un' by Ken Booker, the local coal merchant and village greengrocer.

The two women busied themselves with the daily work; the cleaning, cooking and tidying up a cottage which always seemed to need doing. The older woman was in a similar situation to her daughter..... separated. Years had passed while they lived as vagabonds and now they were thrown together; mother and daughter, with two youngsters to bring up: the young boy and his younger sister.

Many of his earliest memories were of times spent with his Granny or his Nan as she liked to be called. In her quiet moments, as she touched the crown of his head with her fingers, then his forehead, then his eyes, then nose, then mouth, then throat he told her magical tale:

'This is where the Coachman sits,

This is where he cracks his whip,

Eye-winker, Tom Tinker

Nose dropper, Mouth-eater

Chip chopper, chip chopper!'

On wet and stormy nights the crashing of thunder and whiteness of the lightning were merely, "Peter and Paul playing football." His fears were always allayed.

 On one particular morning the rain lay in puddles across the pathway which led to the outside toilet. The bubbling river beyond was swollen and angry. This morning, there were no tugs and barges carrying their brilliant white cargoes of pulp for the paper mills of Aylesford. He had quickly dressed and was on his way to the village school. His mother had already found employment at an engineering factory in the nearby city of Rochester and was away hours before on the early shift.

His grandmother waved him off. 'Ye take care; mind yerself,' she intoned in her kindly Irish accent. She wore a triangular scarf on her head to cover her thinning hair. He waved and his heart warmed and his step quickened with her words.

Today was a day he would always remember. It was the one on which his teacher, Mrs. Pole, took him aside and told him he was ready to be taught to read. Both the Head teacher and Mrs. Pole thought this a good idea, so in the quiet corridor away from the classroom the irrepressible and gifted Mrs. Pole set about her magic. Within the shortest of times he could recognise the simplest of words and so he could join his classmates.

They were a mixed group from around the village. There were the Fleming twin girls, crazy Barry Cornwall who whirly gigged every playtime and knocked everyone down, there was his friend Billy, and the giant Kevin Bleen and a few Burrants from the large family across the road from his Wouldham house.

During this time he thought little of his father. He had gone away before and he always came back, even if it was to argue and shout with his mother. Instead, the rough land around the cottage and the river came to dominate his thoughts. People seemed to matter less than places or things- except for Crockett. Davy Crockett was the exception to the boy's rule as the backwoodsman headed up the pantheon of heroes which now ruled the boy's life.

Crockett came along via a Disney book and by a song. The boy longed for Tennessee; he craved a fur hat with a raccoon tail and the forests and woods of the southern United States. Above all, Crockett was masterful, strong, free and resourceful. He understood the forests and the little brooks and streams. He could listen in and understand Native Americans.

Crockett was a man of his word – a man who could survive against any odds- a man who could 'wrastle barrs, talk to 'critters', understand the sounds and smells and signs of the forest.

This new and developing situation of almost suspended animation continued for some time. His kindly but at times feisty grandmother stayed at home with his sister; and his hard working and caring mother, working hard and hurrying away to her new job at the local engineering works. His mother came home tired and always smelled of oil.

It was a long way from rural Meath where her own grandmother and two uncles still lived or the rugged stony ground of Scrigg, in Mayo, where she went to school. But she was hardy and adaptable and seemed to get used to the harshness of factory life. Before the job, she never used to smell of oil but in time the factory had claimed her as one of its own. For the boy, it signalled a change even though the extraordinariness of some everyday events sometimes militated against the sensation of timelessness and stasis.

Events like the appearance of a mouse in the box of Scots porridge oats; the yelling and screaming, ending in the incineration of the oats; the box, and the mouse on the little cottage fire. Consider the robin which carelessly flew into the window pane and which was roused from its stunned state and flew away once more. Still his father did not return.

The cottage was snug and warm, as firework night and the winter approached. That winter eventually passed and the spring brought many changes to his regular and predictable daily routine. His mother had a visitor: a young man, tall and with wavy brown hair. He drove a smart green Singer sports car and seemed very interested in everyone. Soon he was a very regular visitor and the boy knew they were 'courting'.

The young man, Gerald, seemed fun. He played with the young boy; teased him with jokes; and even tied him up with a challenge to escape. He felt then that the young man consciously wanted to be friends with him; like an older brother who could take him into his confidence, but the boy was already too far down the line. He understood what his father had done and now realised that he had to sit still and wait and tough it out and it would all come out well.

The boy knew that his mother was fond of her younger work colleague, but there was little her son could do about it. Jealousy and irritation crept in. The boy came to dislike the visits because he knew it as a time of losing touch with his mother. Up until then, all her attention had been upon him and his sister. He still felt he was the special one; the special one who had chosen a course for his young life. He felt himself to be the one who had been through the difficult times, with his mother; the one who had contributed to and had shared her troubles.

One day his mother was going out with Gerald. The boy wanted to know what they were going to do and where they were going. Knowing what was happening was important and empowering for him.

'Where are you going?' he cut in, 'where are you going?' 'To see a man about a dog,' retorted his mother and laughed a horrible grown up laugh.

Gerald put his arm around her shoulder and chuckled. She was wearing her green cardigan with the black poodle motif and with her dark red hair she looked like a film star. As a young woman it was said she had modelled for knitting-pattern company.

The boy felt proud of her but felt, with a sense of inevitability that she was slipping away from him. The charming Gerald was on the scene and the convertible Singer sports car life was something his mother had never experienced with his father. Their lives had been angry and fractious and in the end, without hope. Of course his mother wanted a good life and she deserved something better than his own father had been able to provide.

The courtship, the registry office wedding in Maidstone, where the boy was the 'page' was soon in the past. Almost overnight they were on the move to their new council house on the corner of the estate and alongside the alleyway. It was a village further along the Medway valley where new homes sprung up on a green field site.

The semi detached house was spacious, clean and modern for its day. It had mains gas, a new cooker and a copper washer with chunky wooden tongs. The front room had dark brown vinyl tiles which were serviceable but not attractive. The boy had his own room and his sister had her own room; things were looking up. He changed schools and moved into his new infant school's senior class with the Headmistress, Miss Jones. She liked the boy because he wanted to learn but she unnerved him with her stern face and severe gold rimmed glasses.

He loved school, learning came easily and enjoyably. Above all, he was popular. Girls liked his freckled face and his energy. He was elusive and funny and never stayed still for long; always onto the next thing.

His Grandmother came with them and stayed initially, but she too was on the move with her job done and her own living to make. She moved from Kent to West London to work for the Americans that she loved. Both his grandmother and his mother would get together for their rare trips back to Ireland on the train and ferry.

In 1958 his half sister came along. It was a home birth and the house was busy on the day. The excitement was high, especially for his new stepfather who looked anxious and paced around without purpose. It was particularly noticeable that on that day the dynamics were changing. The centre of gravity started to move inexorably away from him and his sister, and towards his new, beautiful half sister. There were the early pains of him being less important than he had been; of moving a little further from the centre and to the edge. He found himself looking in from the edge, helping and listening. He began to look outwards from his family and the new world of the new estate and its inhabitants began to come to prominence; but he also looked inwards at the history of his recent past. In that past he found strength, conviction and purpose.

Over the next few years he threw himself into the 'real world'; things physical or from the surrounding countryside. Football and cricket came to rule his world; and he spent less and less time in the home. The home was dull and he was restless and anxious. The dreams which had dominated his early time ebbed away. The ploughman dream had ended.

His father had not returned. He had heard nothing. There had been no contact. He still felt like his father's son. It couldn't be any other way. He was and perhaps would always be in another family and couldn't let go.

Sometimes he seemed to adjust to the new way, 'codding' himself that this new young man, a couple of years younger than his mother, could pick up where his natural father had left off. The boy gave this so much effort. He tried so hard to pretend that his early life had not really existed. Trying to imagine that this young fresh faced young man had always been there for him and the earlier memories were part of his imagination.

In the new house with its cream, clean distempered walls, any talk of the old house or the old days, or especially of his father was totally forbidden. Those chalky walls had no writing upon them; no record of what had gone before. They represented the new start, the fresh cream board, the 'tabular rasa' ready for him to write upon or for someone else to write upon.

His previous life soon became a taboo subject. Something which was there, but could be never mentioned. It was this intense secrecy about the past which challenged the boy the most. At that time he was too young and enmeshed to understand the changes they were wishing upon him. For him it was a battle with others about his identity. It was becoming submerged below the waterline of the new life that Gerald and his mother were creating for themselves and their family. But if all the stuff of memory had not existed, as his mother claimed, then who was he? What was he? What was his identity now if all those things which made him so far, were denied?

The boy began to realise that his father would never return and that he would have to adjust to the new order. It was not a comfortable place to be. He had energy and knowledge and memory which carried him onwards and onwards. Any who showed interest in him he liked. He was so easily flattered and compliant with those he thought loved him. At school he thrived on praise and wilted under criticism. To achieve praise and above all 'admiration' meant work and being surprising; knowing things and reading things and doing things that his class mates never did.

The driver during these days was the search for praise and admiration and defiance- on the sports field or on the cross country circuit track; or on the football pitch. It was at this time, in the early days at the new house that changing the story- such as Gerald was at his birth; he held him and watched his first steps His mother forgot about everything. She lied and she blanked the stuff of life and always would. His biological father was 'no good.' The boy didn't know him.

His own mother had destroyed all records of her husband after the separation. There was no such thing as access. There were no photographs, no images whatsoever, except those in the boy's head. His real father had become a nonperson. But the fact that those images could not be expunged entirely would mean they would become a force factor throughout his future life. Mother must have been so annihilated by the relationship that it led her to a cataclysmic break down.

Later he would come to understand that his father had let him down; left him abandoned upon this rock of life; crashed in upon by the cruel seas and shoals of predators. He had to find his identity. Any academic failures were catastrophic because they showed him to be as useless as his father- unable to support a wife and children and to provide for them.

Gerald could do that. He had a good education and had landed a steady job at the diesel pump works. He was bright, methodical and calculating. He could provide security and stability. What he couldn't do was to take over where his own father, for all his faults had left off. Only the real thing could do that.

Gerald knew all this, but the boy's mother believed deeply in her new husband on and awarded him a generous reservoir of emotional intelligence. At that time, it was something he alone could not develop with his step son.

For the boy, it wasn't that he didn't love his mother. He loved her with every fibre of his being. Didn't he choose her over his father? Had she always been there for him as they say? But he hated her behaviour; the secrecy; the illusion; the fabrication and lies; the cover up and pretence; ...it was all badly handled. They had more important work to do bringing up the young baby daughter and rightly, much of 1958 was spent rearing the new child.

By the middle of the following year there was talk of names, papers, adoptions and such like. His mother and Gerald wanted all the children to have the same name. His sister, Kiera was keen to shift from the blunt and ugly name of Dobbs to the sophisticated, romantic or pretentious sounding Devreaux. Who would have a name like Devreaux in a village like ours? Kiera never liked their father's original name anyway. In fact she hated the name and even in later years found it hard to enunciate it without stumbling over the crude sounds.

Kiera wanted to change. She was about to move up into the primary school at Aylesford and it was opportune. She was wisely compliant and in her willow way bowed with any breeze. 'Devreaux' she mouthed to herself in her mirror, 'Devreaux,' it suited her purpose well.

For the boy it was an altogether different issue. In his view, changing his name was a betrayal of his father; a renunciation of his existence. Somewhere in him, the bright flame of loyalty and love and sentiment would continue to burn and torture him. If his father were to come back, then what? How could they be together again? A name is an identity; a piece of who we are and who we came from. Who is a name really for?

His mother was adamant. The name should be changed. Why wouldn't he want the new name? For his mother, the continued existence of his original name was a constant reminder of the failed marriage; a constant shadow of her previous existence. Why wouldn't he want to change? His own sister had become a Devreaux!

His mother explained that he wouldn't be legally adopted. Being adopted was financially out of reach and pointless. He wouldn't be adopted by his new step father. The boy could just 'assume' the new name...he would from now on be known as John Devreaux. His new school could change it in their registers. Usage would make the new name acceptable. It would only be a matter of time. You needn't go through solicitors and such like. They were not for us. So John Dobbs made the shift to John Devreaux.

Despite his efforts, the boys at the school were merciless. A few footballers from the school team worst of all. In corridors. Inside the six yard box. Uniformed boys, passing him by in the cloakrooms and changing rooms rang out with ' OK Dobbsy ; 'what the hell is Devreaux, Dobbsy?' 'What sort of name is that?' Your name's Dobbsy, you prat'   'Oi Dobbsy. I've heard you're a bastard with no father!' 'Where's that name from? It's foreign ain't it?

It was the footballers who hurt the most. Teachers were circumspect; staying clear of something they didn't understand. The footballers were different, so there were fights. Plenty of them. Some spiteful and nasty; others ending in, 'I'm only joking.' Those that had an axe to grind with petty jealousies continued to hack into him.

At home things were little better. After he had agreed to change his name, his mother had given him instructions to take all references to his old name from all his old books, reports and certificates. Grudgingly and with much deep sadness he cut out 'Dobbs' from swimming certificates, from countless school reports, from a certificate for an essay in a Cadbury's competition, from his old cub certificates and his cycling proficiency.

His mother helped him to carefully cut out the references to Dobbs. Of course the certificates all looked rather strange with little rectangular inserts of the new name placed in the cut out windows. For the new boy, John Devreaux, it felt like cutting off his own air supply.

He had to reinvent himself. It had been eight or ten years since his father had gone. Devreaux was becoming established but his step father struggled to work with him.

At times the two could work together decorating the house for all hours; or lift the thousands of flints which chequered the rough garden. At times they were close; but they were never alike. They were different in their values, their priorities and their aims in life.

If they had been blood; then the chemistry would work. But they were not and however hard they both worked at the relationship it would always prove to be difficult. Even the fun of the 'winged wheel' and the Velocette, the BSA C15 and the steady stream of Ford

Popular and Ford Consul cars which stole his heart but could not make much long term difference to his stern logic.

He was his father's son and it was an inescapable fact. His father had not returned and he easily assumed that he did not care about him or know where he lived or knew of his change of name. How would he find him if he had changed his name? How would he know where to look? The handful of memories played with his senses and unbalanced him.

Only in activity did he lose himself. Only in the endless hurly burly did the dull ache and the injustice in his life ease away. His sister began to not matter. She had slotted herself in to the new order and for her it all worked well. She was naturally compliant even frail in adversity.

In his mind, she had 'gone over' to the other side and at times was 'one of them'. This hurt him. She slotted in and he did not and forever this would be a source of pain and loss. He knew he would never feel quite the same about her. He felt less protective of her and she felt more of a stranger to him. Photographs at that time find him standing alone; on a beach or outside the British Museum; the last boy hanging on to a series of long gone memories.

In those early days he certainly felt a sense of guilt; that he was in some mysterious way responsible for what had happened. He fantasised that if he had done this or that or avoided this or that, then all would be saved. Things would revert back. The happy family would re-emerge from this confusion and he would resort back to his old ways in charge. Only later did he realise that it was the best thing that could have happened and that the new man had probably saved his sister and himself from going into care. The imminent move by the new man to the new house, in the new village lay ahead.

2. Wild and Free

It was about 1957 when the Field family moved in next door to us and took up residence at 41 Greengrass Close. My parents, sister and I had moved from our tumbledown cottage in Wouldham village to a new estate in Eccles. Our new semi-detached council house was a beautiful and sparkling three bed roomed property.

We had been there a few months when a removal van arrived with our new, next door neighbours, Mr and Mrs Field and their two teenage children Eileen and David. Mrs Field looked rather like an old fashioned school mistress, while Mr Field physically resembled a morphed version of Albert Einstein.

It turned out that both Eileen and David worked in the nearby town of Maidstone but the parents were retired and spent most of their time at home. The parents rarely came out of the house but we had managed some nodding contact and a few 'good mornings' to Mrs Field.

Mr Field was altogether a more elusive creature and rarely came out into his very overgrown back garden and if he did, and I called over, he rarely acknowledged my greeting and I found that quite hard to understand. Did he not care? Was I just a tedious kid?

Mr Field started to become the focus of my attention and that wasn't a particularly good thing for Mr F. because I could be a dogged nuisance, always alert to events and constantly developing plans and schemes to get to the bottom of 'what is going on?'

Fortunately my bedroom window overlooked the front of our house and gave me a clear view of the close outside.

At this time I was an 'Airfix' kit addict on an indomitable journey building Dornier bombers, Messerschmitt 109s, Spitfires and Hurricanes, so I spent a reasonable amount of time in my bedroom especially when the weather was wet or cold.

It was from the room that I made my first disquieting observation and this is what happened: it was a warm summer's evening and I had been asleep in my bed, with the windows open and the curtains pulled back. The plastic 'planes were moving gently on their ceiling strings when, at about 2.30 in the morning, I could hear the scrape of metal on the road outside.

I crept out of bed and made my way across to the window and cautiously peeped out. I could see Mr Field carrying his dustbin out onto the street where he began tipping the contents, mainly ash from his fire, onto the road. I couldn't, for the life of me, understand why he was doing this. Next he stood the dustbin up and disappeared for a minute or two. I could see the pile of ash and the dustbin beside it.

A few moments later Mr Field appeared again, this time with a broom and shovel and proceeded to sweep the ash onto the shovel and pop it back into the dustbin. Absolutely extraordinary! To my inexperienced, child's mind, his actions seemed to serve no useful purpose and that bothered me all night.

In the morning I told my parents what I had seen in the night and then the truth came out. They had spoken to Mrs Field and had been told that her husband had suffered a terrible injury in a road accident where his skull had been broken and then patched up with a metal plate. In my mind the image of a piece of metal attached to one's head seemed to me to be grossly unnatural, but it was thought this might explain his erratic behaviour. Nonetheless, it had the opposite effect on me. Rather than turn me away from my interest in Mr Field, it actually stimulated my imagination and curiosity further. From then on I observed him at every opportunity and his erratic and ultimately unhappy behaviour eventually turned me away from my sleuth mentality.

Some years after I had moved from Eccles and at about 2.30 in the morning in fact, I was returning home to Strood. I always motorcycled along the top road above Wouldham. Some 4 miles from my old village, I passed a man with his wild hair blowing, his scarf around his neck, striding into the brightness of my headlights, looking like another Einstein: It was Mr Field, wild and free!

3. The Estate (1)

When we moved into Greengrass Close in 1957, it was a momentous occasion for our family. Imagine moving from a damp, dilapidated, tumbledown cottage, with its outdoor toilet with neatly strung squares of newspaper in place of toilet paper; with our old tin bath; to a brand new house on a sparkling new council estate. This would be our home for the next six years and at first all was well with the world.

The estate had been built on a green field site on the edge of Eccles village and the parts of fields we now called our garden, had once been fields of corn or wheat in earlier days. However, on our magnificent corner plot we had a problem, endemic to the area-flints! We excavated piles and piles of knobbly blue, grey and brown flint stones; piles which stood taller than I, all tugged and dug and wrenched from the soil.

Mother wanted the garden cleared and prepared for some shrubs in the borders which would surround the lawns; and for the planting of vegetables to supplement both diet and income. Grandfather, George came from Sittingbourne in his beige Hillman Minx, to dig and plant and to weed and do battle with the ubiquitous flints. However, it would be wrong to have relied entirely on Grandfather, especially when Mr Brown at number 39 was retired, but willing to help for a few shillings.

Mr Brown wore an armful of tattoos with all sorts of messages, but beneath the pictures he was a man of few words. He had served in the navy and his roaming days were over and it seemed that his main worry was his predatory daughter. It was she who frequented Chatham dockyard, always with a variety of sailors. Her own picturesque arms told their own story in dark blues and reds; fascinating for a ten year old.

The estate was quickly populated with rambling families of Bonners, and Davises and smaller families of Andersons, Moores, Goldings, Norrises, Wilsons, Tuppers, Humphreys, Huggins, Lowes, Boozers, Geddes, Suttons, Salmons, Beadles, Austins, Babins and Germaneys.

The younger children from the estate swarmed into the village school at the end of Eccles Row; the older children attended Primary schools at Burham or Aylesford.

It was on the estate that I met Geoffrey Hunter and for us it was so busy in the close, we would stand on Bull Lane collecting car registration numbers! That calmed us down. We also had this odd arrangement whereby he and I captured newts, mainly great crested and palmate, and he took them to a pet shop in Maidstone, redeeming them for a few shillings in cash!

We spent many an hour stalking elusive lizards, slippery frogs, great-crested newts and of course, the ever popular grass snakes. One day he arrived carrying a cloth bag with a draw string.

'Put your hand in,' he grinned.

'What's in there?'

'An adder!' he said and laughed and laughed.

There was always something afoot. Gossip was rife and whispers many. We were scrumping apples in season; and the farmer was bent on scaring us off by firing his twelve bore over our heads and in our direction. On one visit I remember, Westwell's orchard was full of bulls, busily browsing the lush grass beneath the trees.

'Let's see if we can get up the trees, get the apples and leg it!' said my friend Kevin.

We scrambled over the farmer's fence and hurried to our chosen trees. The bulls were very interested. They stood below our perches and stubbornly refused to move, trapping us on the boughs. Never underestimate a bull!

I challenged Kevin to put an apple on the nearest one's horn, but I don't think he understood my drift; so hanging down from the apple bough I managed to force the apple on to the beast's curving horn; and then I did it a second time. Bulls with apples on their horns; what a gas! What a picture!

On another jape, using our bikes, a flock of us would ambush the tractor and cart which carried fresh peas, still in their pods. We would hover behind the cart, like a swarm of hornets, and reach forward and grab handfuls of the shiny green pods before thrusting them up under our jackets. At last, near the old oast house, we sat down beside the road and munched them up.

Mackender's Lane was the place to be. Some days I envied Gary Drayton, on the lane, at his piano lessons; and can still see myself standing and gawping through the window, listening to him playing and wishing it was me!

 Then there was the unwelcome building work being done opposite the alley. The wolf whistling labourers were clearing our ancient cherry orchard and were building yet another estate. There would be no more rich velvet cherries to pick and savour. No more woodpeckers hammering and boring into the trees to nest; only the unending banter of the young labourers encouraging and coaxing clever and willing Jennie Messey into their site caravan. Soon, she would be carrying a bump in front of her, as proof of their attentions and the onward march of progress.

Along the far end of the lane stood the 'Red Cow' public house and it was where Mr McFadden our estate neighbour, originally from Kirkcudbrightshire, drank his stout. Like many of his generation, the war was still a common topic for pub talk. The living proof was my giant school friend, Edward Gunter, whose father had been a German prisoner who stayed on in England after the war.

Occasionally both McFadden and Gunter drank with one of the most seriously mysterious men in our village, Mr Parrot. Mysterious? Firstly there was his name. For a ten year old, 'Parrot' took some believing. Is this old guy kidding me? Parrot? Mr Parrot?

Old Mr Parrot worked as a farm labourer and could be found in the ancient dilapidated barn opposite the top end of the recreation ground. Like a lone gambler he shuffled the bales of straw around, staying until darkness when bats drove him out and random noises frightened him.

'Were you in the war, Mr Parrot?' I asked him one day.

'Yep', he replied. 'Was it in the war that you lost your ear?'

'Aha, in the war.' 'Was it the First war?'

'Yep, a bullet in the war.'

'Did it hurt Mr Parrot?'

Mr Parrot turned away with no expression at all on his face. He hauled up the next bale of straw and stacked it methodically upon the other bales. We never spoke again.

4. The Estate (2)

After moving from Wouldham, our next school was to be Eccles Infants and the headmistress was Mrs Smith. My sister, three years my junior, went into the youngest class and I into the older class. I sat a lot with Larry Betts playing draughts and a simple game called 'three in a row'.

Every morning, our first task was to complete our daily diary. It told the ongoing story about what was happening to us at that time and what we were doing. Each half page was illustrated with a picture. I know you might laugh at this, but my diary had more than its fair share of pictures which declared:

'This is wartime'. It did seem to be a childish 'get out sentence' when little was happening at home.

At break in the school, we walked on empty syrup tins which were pierced and threaded with string and used for stilts. Even from my point of view it felt makeshift but could be fun.

On one occasion my sister Kiera offended the Head Teacher by playing in the sand pit when the youngest pupils were not allowed near the sink which contained the sand. Mrs Smith stood her in the corner as a punishment. That was where I found her, sobbing.

I went to the Head Teacher and began to plead my sister's case; how she was new and didn't know the rules; how she would never be deliberately difficult and how she was upset. Miraculously she was released and had learned her lesson.

It was here that pupils learned to get along with each other and of course to establish the pecking order. As afternoons came and went in stories and music and poetry I dreamed and left the world.

In my mind I could see the misty gentle curve of the churned up khaki brown waters; the wavelets drifting irresistibly in the breeze; and on the surface were the grey mullet coming up the river from east to west.

 The mullet were swimming up the rich Medway waters and I was poaching with Peter. We were hidden in the reeds, our two heads bobbing and moving in the final preparations for catching the new visitors.

'We ain't gunna catch 'em wiv' bait an normal tackle, so we're gunna afto foul 'ook 'em.'

To this purpose, we had tied triple pike hooks and lead weights onto the tackle and the knack was to cast out the rig as far as possible into the shoal of fish, coming upstream, and to quickly reel in, with the intention of foul hooking the prey.

But why use such a cruel method of catching a fish? Peter reckoned the mullet had soft lips and traditional size 10 hooks would tear away or be deliberately spat out. The wrap around finality of foul hooking would be far more effective.

Peter Sabine reckoned that his father was French Canadian but that didn't matter, I was no General Wolfe. He was my poaching pal at Furnham Lake. We caught the tricky brown and rainbow trout that played out their days in the reservoir's clear waters. Sabine and I always fished at night and avoided the bailiff and his enthusiastic Alsatian dog.

I never liked resorting to poaching and had even gone to the trouble of writing a nice letter to the water company which owned the reservoir, only to receive a belligerent response which dented my faith somewhat and set me on the poacher's path.

Sometimes we got tangled up, our lines broke, we were 'done in.' We couldn't afford to lose our tackle; rather we would strip down to our pants and go down into the cold lake waters to get the tackle back. Swimming down there was risky but essential.

Over in the destroyed cement works we finished our mornings, catching great crested and palmate newts, not for money but just for fun.

5. <u>The Estate</u> (3)

At the start of our time on the estate, everything was new and exciting. We had a new copper with wooden tongs for boiling up our washing; an elegant mains gas cooker; tiled floors throughout the living room; new taps and fittings; indoor toilets and our own rooms! Of course, we were followed by the cylindrical paraffin heaters, which stood at the top of the stairs and in the hallway; causing the whole place to smell faintly of paraffin.

Tradesmen came around the block and paraded their wares on the estate: the pink paraffin man, the Esso blue dealer, the Walls ice cream man, the Corona, Tizer and R.Whites lemonade vendors, the vegetable seller, coalman and seafood man.

Step father, Gerald started out enthusiastically to work at C.A.V. on his red bicycle for the days of the Singer sports car were gone. However, he quickly realised it would be difficult during the winter to get to his work on the Esplanade, Rochester, so he quickly upgraded to a BSA 'winged wheel' cyclemotor. Now this form of transport was a cross between a cycle and a moped and gave the rider some assistance when needed.

It sufficed for a few months but proved to be a strenuous form of transport, not much better than a cycle, so it ended its days in the garden shed.

His next bike was an iconic Velocette, a gift from his father. Often used by the police, it was virtually silent and difficult to identify in its understated grey livery.

Next came the BSA C15 in a lovely green and with as distinctive a sound as a Spitfire. Step father wore his white helmet and visor; black Belstaff jacket; and black leather gauntlets. He loved the motorcycle, except in the depths of winter and it was a severe winter in December 1962 through to January 1963. Brutal winds blew the settled snow for days on end. The result was huge snow drifts like unruly white monsters clinging to our houses. Snow had accumulated above our front door right up under the bedroom windows. All travel was by foot and gradually the village came to a halt.

The sea had frozen in Herne Bay; a double-decker bus had careered off the road in Wouldham. Passengers hacked their way on foot to their villages. Finally, the village of Eccles was cut off. We were trapped indoors, all traffic ceased and outdoor life ground slowly to a halt.

On our television, hazy black and white pictures of helicopters, dropping straw and feed for the beleaguered animals on Dartmoor were broadcast; rivers were frozen; trees were laden with snow; roads were beyond treacherous; abandoned vehicles were everywhere and the estate's children were out in it, hyper-excited, enjoying their extra time off school in a new world controlled by nature and not by adults!

The hard winter finished stepfather's romance with the motorcycle. Enter VUV 843, a Ford Anglia, which soon proved to have a 'cracked block'. Enter 580 BKO, the beige Ford Consul.

When we returned to school again it was to the first tranche of a new vaccine to combat the sinister poliomyelitis outbreak. Rational thought seemed to take a back seat while the disease strangled our sanity. Mother ordered us to avoid drains at all times, because somehow the disease lurked down there, underground, waiting for an unsuspecting child to wander by, inhale, and then develop signs of the disease. We were in a state of panic about the outbreak of this hidden monster, especially since we had already been exposed to its consequences. Let me tell you how this happened.

My Irish Grandmother worked as housekeeper for an American family in north London. Her employer was a Lieutenant in the U.S air force and the couple had two young sons. To be sure, Nan loved Americans, ever since she had lived and married in New York. She loved their cars, Betty Crocker cakes and their attitude to life. On one weekend we were invited to visit.

Midway through the afternoon my mother, stepfather and I were taken into an annex to visit the Lieutenant's mother who had been damaged by polio, the disease we all feared. In the middle of the room appeared to be a long metal cylinder.

"My Mom's in an 'iron lung.' It keeps her going....."

The machine, as if responding to the Lieutenant, gave out a whoosh at the rear, as the bellows sucked the air in and out of the casing. The machine looked truly shocking with its long, metal, coffin-like tube, and with what appeared to be a disembodied human head projecting from one end.

He approached the head. The woman moved a little and gave her son a wry smile. He stroked her hair tenderly and respectfully but said nothing to her.

"Polio," he said grimly. We all nodded.

I left the scene with a couple of nice American shirts, one with a wagon wheel motif, the other with a Crocket theme and... a red and blue plastic rocket which, when half filled with water and pumped with air, would fly around the school playground like a demented doodle bug! I also left with the image of a silver sarcophagus tattooed on my brain.

That summer holiday we played test matches of three or four day duration on the recreation ground. Adam Loxley provided the bats; I had some homemade pads; and for posterity, Rich kept a written record of each innings. Others like Gunter, Cookie, Frobisher and more joined in. We batted like Barrington and Cowdrey just then.

An old combine harvester had been abandoned by Farmer Westwell at the edge of the rec' and at the end of every test match we all sat up there and read out and discussed the results.

One evening we were all up on the harvester, when Gavin Westwell, the farmer's eighteen year old son, came along. He was affronted by we test cricketers sitting up there on his father's rusty combine and took particular exception to my remark that the machine seemed to have been abandoned for months. We all apologised for the misunderstanding and got down from the rig but it wasn't enough for him.

He came straight at me and smashed me in the face with his fist. I seemed to have an age to decide whether or not to retaliate. Against my nature, I decided that any physical response from me would result in a greater beating. A second and third punch and fourth blow connected with my mouth and chin and nose. I took the barrage. A voice screamed out. Old Mr Paddel, the village butcher came to my rescue, and Westwell stopped his assault.

"Leave him alone, you bully! Pick on someone your own age," The old, balding butcher, yelled his curse to the back of Westwell's head as the teenager walked away.

During our rest days Rich and I set up a Bell's telephone link between numbers 43 and 59 ; we electrified my garden fence with a makeshift adapted conductor; we interrupted the pesky teenagers who walked by with transistor radios by jamming their wavelengths. We camped in the back garden and tried to encourage Mollie Copping to join us, but with no success.

The regular tests of strength or fights on the recreation ground still continued and the rules were always the same. One against one; the village way. The crowd kept out of it and ensured that no other boy got involved. Each tournament usually ended with the two adversaries becoming the best of friends.

I know I'm jumping the gun, but by the time we moved to Strood and closer to father's workplace, we had to clear out everything, even our adorable cat, Tigger. We could not take him with us and so, "he would have to be 'put to sleep.' "

We kids argued, but it was futile. I raged and battled for 'Tigger Bomb Cat's' life but it was hopeless. I loved that cat. He was a ginger giant, too proud to take down. But my parents were securely focussed on the exchange of houses they had planned- until I came up with my own secret solution - abduction!

On the final Saturday before our moving date, and at about three thirty in the morning, I crept stealthily out of bed and went down to the place where Tigger Bomb Cat hung out, or rather, stretched out. I had hidden a rucksack and with some difficulty had TBC in the bag, as they say. In the darkness I unlocked our shed, took out the trusty cycle and off I went towards Aylesford.

I cycled about four or five miles that morning across the fields and towards the furthest part of that village. It was there, sadly and solemnly, with strokes and hugs, I released my beloved cat.

No one suspected a thing. I was home and in bed again ready to be woken on Saturday morning. I forgot all about TBC and knew he would be fine. He was a survivor, a great ginger giant. That cat would make friends and live!

In the late afternoon, I went down to the recreation ground with Rich, to bowl a few overs at Loxley and curiously the combine harvester was gone. I told them the story about 'acting the ape,' at school, when we had a film about primates- chimps- I think, and a few of the boys started mimicking chimp behaviour. I liked to imitate a chimp peeling and eating a banana and to be fair to her, the adorable Miss Sparks, our teacher, warned me enough not to behave this way.

At the end of her tether, she kept me back for detention and at the end of school she took me to the hall and stood me in front of the mirror there.

'Now peel some pretend bananas John, and make as many monkey faces in the mirror as you like. I'll be back in half an hour.' She forgot about me.

About an hour later, the Headmaster came along.

'What on earth are you doing, young man?'

'Monkey behaviour, sir'

'Go home!' said the Headmaster. Adam Loxley laughed and balanced the cricket ball on the back of his hand.

I returned about six o'clock and got a telling off for missing tea. Mum brought me a glass of milk and I gulped it down. I stood up for a second filling and there, asleep on the chair was Tigger Bomb Cat.

6. The Witch Of Mackender's Lane

Mackender's Lane was a magical place when I was young. It lay adjacent to a narrow alley where I had slammed my head into the fence and been stitched up, without anaesthetic, by Doctor Binder, on our round kitchen table at 43, Greengrass Close.

On one side of this alley were allotments and on the other side a longish drive leading to two conjoined cottages.

Opposite the junction between the alley and Mackender's Lane was an orchard of aged cherry trees and further towards the 'Red Cow' public house were two fine Victorian properties and beside them Abraham Burrell's builder's yard.

In a bungalow, in the opposite direction lived my friend Cliff Edwards. His father had tried to teach us how to use Morse code but we were too wild and restless to learn such a disciplined series of dashes and dots.

Beyond Edwards' bungalow were masses of cherry laurel bushes. This was important because I knew that a collection of the leaves, cut into strips and placed in the bottom of a vessel would make an effective 'killing jar' for the insect specimens I collected.

Anyway, opposite the glossy cherry laurel ran an alleyway between houses; and beside the alleyway in a lonely house lived a witch.

For me, at the age of 10, witches had to meet a set of simple criteria. This included: white hair, dark eyes, thin haggard faces, slightly hunched backs and in this case, the owner of a besom broom. We were positive about her. We were the inquisitors who had found this little wizened lady, a real reclusive witch, hiding in the lane in her secretive little castle; hiding from us. She spooked Rich and I to our bones, but we were going to test her out in our childish way.

Stoning must be a very elementary response from human beings, even young and mischievous ones like Rich and I, for it was 'stoning' that we did every time we passed her house.

'Peg a few flints at her garage,' I said. Rich was less keen.

Anyway, I scrabbled about for a couple of decent sized knobs of flint ammunition and lobbed a few in the direction of the witch's outbuilding. Magically, out she came, waving her besom in the air and shouting incoherently in strange tongues. But she knew we had found her out. She knew she was cornered and she knew she had to plot her revenge!

Some few weeks passed and Rich and I were up to other things in the village. However, on an idle Saturday afternoon we passed the witch's house and bombarded the drive and outbuilding with our homemade flint mortars and grenades. Big mistake! We had pestered her too much.

Confident and without hesitation she emerged from her little fortress. She started remonstrating with us and shook her scrawny fist in the air. Rich and I started running along the lane towards the alley and the sanctuary of our respective homes.

As we turned into the safety of the alley, we looked over our shoulders and like the supernatural being that she was, the old witch was still following us.

Now being followed by a witch is a horrible experience for any 10 year old and whatever the experts say, a witch is one of the most dogged, persistent and ruthless stalkers ever known. We were terrified.

At the top of the alley I dived through the gate of 43 and through the side door and up the stairs. Rich hacked on to the shelter of number 59.

I went straight to my room and peered out behind the curtain. Sure enough the witch materialised at my front door and I could hear my parents speaking with her. Typically, she had bewitched them into believing her story and had woven her magic around them, no doubt leaving me high and dry, without even my parents as allies. I was called down for the inquisition.

'John, John! Come down here!' yelled my Mum, more puzzled than angry. 'What have you been doing? Mrs Whitlake says you have been throwing stones at her garage. Have you?'

There comes a point, in the affairs of boys, where honesty is definitely the best policy! ' I have,' I blurted out, 'I'm sorry. I shouldn't have.'

The witch snapped, 'why did you pick on me? What did I ever do to you?'

My witch story did not now seem to be a reasonable response to her pretty fair question. I fell silent.

'Well,' she continued, pointing at me with her wand like finger, 'the next time you are in Mackenders Lane, your parents would like you and your friend to stop by and come into the house and we can try to get along with each other a little better.'

For me this did not seem to be a particularly helpful solution and my apology did not really seem to be an option either, but I tried it nonetheless.

'I am sorry,' I said, 'we'll stop by and visit you.'

Rich was soon consulted and the moment to confront our demon came around.

Rich, 'the Rock' Soloman,' was pleased that he had missed the exhumation of our deeds and was doubly delighted that his parents Barry and Martha had not found out about our churlish behaviour.

Imagine the scene on that windswept, rainy day as we kept our part of the bargain: Rich and I entering the witch's lair, I mean, lounge; being asked what soft drink and what cakes we would like! Further imagine being settled upon her spongy throne-like chairs, surrounded by the high walls of her dungeon, dotted with grey, grainy pictures, of soldiers from the Great War.

Under my breath I mouthed the words, 'deep raspberry blood and slices of grilled toad.'

No, John, be normal. What's normal? Calm, as if you are at home.

'Orange juice please. Vanilla sponge would be nice. Thank you very much'

Mrs Whitlake vanished into her kitchen. I mouthed these words across to Rich. 'What if the drink is poisoned?' I paused and looked towards the doorway. 'Do you reckon the cake is drugged with potions?'

We ate the cake and downed the drink, but the spell she cast on us that day, meant that we never felt the same again; and I must be honest; never again did we trouble the witch of Mackender's Lane.

Route One

Richard Solomon was undoubtedly my best friend from my Eccles days and he would always have a special place in my heart; but on this day our friendship would be tested to the limit, when we decided to climb down, into the excavated chalk pit, from the top of Steer Lane.

One of the things I learned that day was about the softness of chalk and how we were grateful for that fact. So what attracted us there in the first place?

The pit had been used during the war as a firing range, as a place to test and practise with soldiers and tanks. It was easy to find spent cartridges there, but we were regular visitors, not for the ordnance but for the wildlife. It was 'the lost world' for us; a place where we were free to explore and imagine and escape.

At that time there was one entrance through a concealed tunnel shrouded in briars and wild vines. Below our feet were orchids in their dozens. We never told anyone.

Usually we made our way through the dripping tunnel and into a vast flat expanse of grass or 'tundra' as we dubbed it; populated with numerous silver birches surrounding a broad, flat and shallow expanse of water which attracted duck, goose, coot, moorhen, lapwing, partridge, pheasant, quail and even an occasional mute swan.

The waters were criss-crossed with grass snakes and lizards and it was there one day we saw the monster grass snake, many feet in length and the biggest we had ever seen. My friend Gerald Hunter visited regularly with a draw string bag and we caught grass snakes which were in demand from the pet shop in nearby Maidstone. Gerald received a pound for each snake.

Today was different. Rich and I were starting from the top and climbing down. It had to be done, and we wasted no time in getting started. The white cliffs were fringed by a grassy top and our first move was to climb over and latch onto hand holds and foot holds in the nooks and crannies of the chalk. All went well. Rich was quickly below me and making impressive progress down. Perhaps he was finding it too easy.

We were descending cautiously perhaps some sixty feet above the masses of tumbled chalk boulders below, when Rich called out,

'John, I think I'm slipping. I'm losing my footing'

'Hold my ankle' I replied 'until you can adjust yourself,' and at that point Rich grabbed my ankle.

It was that shift in weight and pressure which slowly and inevitably dislodged my own foot from the snug chalk cup that my toes fitted into so nicely. You know how it is, when there's no chance of redemption from an action taken; how there is a blissful bubble moment when you wish you could float, like the dandelion seed, at liberty, to drift without consequences; but the moment simply doesn't materialise.

Rich and I slid face down for some forty feet to the bottom of our 'Lost World' and to be frank, I could not believe that both of us had survived. We were entirely white with chalk powder and in our ghostly garb more than grateful that we had survived, thanks to the softness and kindness of homely chalk. We had also navigated Route One!

8.   Easy Money

In the late 50s and early 60s, wild bird's egg collecting was a 'must do' among Eccles village boys and was not considered for a moment to be against the law or in any way damaging to the environment. Characters like Clive Jury and Steve Delaplace had impressive collections of most birds' eggs from the Kent area. I too had my own collection but nothing to rival Jury and Delaplace.

There was a wide copse of trees which lay beyond Mackender's Lane and in that copse was the tallest elm tree ever. Despite being bombarded by crows, it was to the very top of the elm that I had laboured one day, to collect a crow's egg. Traditionally the collector would carry the egg in the mouth, for safety's sake and to avoid it being 'poshed,' (a popular local word meaning 'smashed'), but on this occasion I would be unable to reach the nest.

It was from that tree that I would plummet- after a rotten branch broke underfoot- causing me to have the most massive fall through the rough bark-body of the tree. At the bottom of that leviathan elm, outside the surrounding brambles, at the very base of the tree, stood Rich.

'John! Are you alright?'

I opened my eyes and moved my toes and arms and legs and head and neck. I was alive. I was scratched, bruised, battered but intact!

'I'm O.K...... Sheesh! That was a hell of a fall!' I groaned.

'Hey Rich, you're not going to believe this .....'

My eyes were then drawn to a small, dusty, collection of .22 calibre live ammunition, near my face, in the dirt under the old elm. It did seem odd that someone left ordnance there but it was ours now. After all, 'possession was nine tenths of the law', or so people said.

Rich and I messed around with the live bullets, carelessly trying to fire them between two flints and eventually becoming bored with our dangerous pastime. I pocketed the bullets and we both wandered across the field towards the far side, where the copse lured us in.

Suddenly a rustling in the brush caught our attention. Weasel? Cat? None of these things! A pigeon!

The pigeon fluttering and flustered tried to evade its inevitable capture, for that is what we were determined upon. It tried to dodge us; it tried to hide and to hunker down in among any weeds or clumps of brush it could find. Its panic was matched with our urgency. Then in an instant I startled it and swept it up against my chest and held it there until it stilled.

'There's a ring on its leg,' yelled Rich. 'Its got a ring.'

'Must be a racing pigeon then, ' I replied, 'I wonder what the colour and number mean?'

'It looks tired out', said Rich, reflecting on the subdued bird.

'It probably had a long journey! Fancy it ending up here!'

'I think Mr Button keeps pigeons. You know, the man who lives at 55. He's got a pigeon loft, I've seen it. He'll know what to do with it.' I responded.

So we went to Mr Button's place and knocked on his front door. I held the pigeon safely, like a professional, with both hands around its wings and body; its feet between my fingers and my jersey over the lot. Known as a quiet man, Mr Button looked surprised and then delighted.

'Ah,' he said 'it's a racing pigeon; gone off its course, perhaps caused by the weather or a predator; but she's a beauty.'

'We thought you could look after her,' Rich chipped in.

'Yes I'll take her,' said Mr Button with a smile.

He reached into his pocket and pulled out a grubby, creased, pound note, 'this is for you,' he grinned.

'Thanks Mr Button,' we warbled happily.

As we closed his gate and headed on to Rich's flat at 59 he turned to me and chimed:

'Easy money, John, easy money! Fancy a game of Subuteo?'

9. The Real Butcher's Boy

At the age of about nine I was fortunate enough to have secured part time employment at Eccles Post Office, delivering newspapers; but, my real calling was to be the Saturday morning 'Butcher's Boy'.

My employer was the balding, ruddy faced Mr Paddel, the village butcher. He was a kind, funny man and his red face comprised of myriads of tiny capillaries at the surface of his skin. His kindness extended to always giving me a few 'chump chops' to take home for my family.

One of my regular Saturday tasks was to cycle to the Carmelite Friary at Aylesford to deliver the regular 56lbs of minced beef to the brothers. It seemed a curious arrangement for me to knock on the oak kitchen door, be met by a monk, and be relieved of the weighty meat from the bike.

The monks shyly mumbled their thanks and while on the return ride, I often wondered how the brothers managed to live in such a secluded way, especially when there was so much for them to see in this beautiful world. The monks seemed introverted and uncommunicative, as if they were simply drifting through this world and were already somewhere else.

When loaded with meat, the bike was a chunky black beast, awkward and heavy, with its rectangular tubular frame on the handlebars. Into those handlebars fitted the rectangular wicker basket and between the cross bar and the 'V' frame were the words:

'J. Paddel, Family Butcher, Eccles, Kent'

My constant worry was falling off, for if that had happened I would not have been able to lift the bicycle up, it being so heavy, especially when filled with minced meat. But once I got back to the shop the real fun started!

I had been trained to use the sausage making machine and spent hours coaxing sausage meat into the pre-made skins. It was a weird process and I have to say, we boys were instructed by Mr Paddel to collect up ALL pieces of spare, waste, off-cut meat. With these miserable offerings (including dry bits and fly bits, from the shop window) we would ensure they found their way into the finished sausages. Yes indeed! Every scrap of fat, meat, gristle, skin, trimming and bluebottle went into the mix!

At the time I worked alongside an older lad named Clive Jury. Clive lived with his parents and brother on Eccles Row, in one of a series of old terraced houses beyond Seer's corner sweet shop. Clive always liked a laugh, especially when Mr Paddel went upstairs for his breakfast, and one of Clive's favourite tricks was locking me in the gigantic meat refrigerator for a while 'to cool down.'

The first time he pushed me into the freezer was pretty scary. It was a large room with a tiled floor and hanging along its length were the carcasses of cattle, pigs, and sheep, dangling on steel 'S' shaped hooks, which in turn were suspended from ceiling rails. When the door was closed and the massive handle thrown across, it was pitch dark and chillingly cold inside. It was a place from which one might never escape!

Clive never locked me in the refrigerator for too long and certainly not long enough to cause real claustrophobia or anxiety; so once I had been tested a few times, he ceased to bother about locking me in the freeze room. It was after passing these tests that Clive accepted me and this was a great thing, for it gave me access to the most knowledgeable boy naturalist in Eccles.

Clive knew everything about every bird, every amphibian, every reptile, and every mammal in the village and in these islands. Clive had the largest collection of bird's eggs, most detailed recognition of flight patterns, habitat and nest building styles of anyone in the village. He was the guru. I hung around to catch his every comment, even those he threw away. Whenever I think of the Red Breasted Merganser I think of Clive Jury, the real butcher's boy.

10. A Big Pair of Shorts

In 1961 many of my friends from Aylesford St Peter's Primary school resided in a place called Pratling Street and to be truthful, they were very friendly, almost clan-like among themselves.

They often messed around at 'The Forstall,' a location which touched the edge of the brown, creamy River Medway. In fact, the surrounding woodland was an unworn, tangled green cloak for boys to dress up in, a place where dreams could be enacted and where fears could be shared.

In the middle was a treacherous piece of swampy ground which my friends, 'giant' Tommy Rice, 'fashionista' Lee Bussel, 'carefree' Robert Cantello and 'serious' David Mitcham advised me to avoid.

'It's dangerous. Don't step into it.'

'No, we can cross that. There're branches and some waste planks; and if we lay them down, form a line and work together we can do it. I'll go first,' I ventured.

The first piece of wood was carefully placed and tentatively, I stepped upon it and it held firm. I wanted to be brave, to prove my worth to these Pratling Street boys. 'Being brave,' not reckless or wilting, was so important then.

'Pass the next.'

Again I stepped out and gingerly transferred my weight from one foot to another. I was light but it still felt unsafe and I began to feel vulnerable, despite the crew behind me.

It was then that I began sinking and sinking, and sinking, steadily and inexorably into the sticky, gluey mud. Now, my friendly reader, sinking into soft, greedy mud is a strange thing; like being slowly drawn down by a slime magnet. It was instantly cool to the skin but seemingly irreversible, inevitable and inanimately hostile.

'I'm going down,' I yelled, 'take my arm; take my arm, pull me out!'

The mud was quickly up to my buttocks. It was the inevitability of what could happen here which spurred me on. Common sense unseated bravery. Foolishness was defeated.

'We've got you John. Hold on.' yelled giant Tommy.

'Pull us back.'   'I've got you' shrieked Lee.

It was a slow motion tug of war and gradually I came out, to a chorus of cheers and a descant of slurps and squelches from the reluctant mud.

Glaring angrily at the mud holed footmarks, curly haired Cantello piped up.

'Sheesh, John, you can't go home like that.'

'Come to my house' said giant Tommy, 'you can wash yourself down and wear a pair of my shorts home.'

That's how I came to arrive home in Eccles, wearing a very big pair of someone else's shorts.

11. Fishing on a Snowy Day.

Why two chumps decide to go fishing, when the gravel pits are frozen over, is now beyond my understanding; and yet this is certainly something my sister Kiera and I did as we were growing up. It became a family incident which she always remembers and often repeats when she has an interested audience, so I will try and relate it for you as accurately as I can.

At the far end of Aylesford's football pitches were two small gravel pits which formed an 'L' shape. The vertical line and the horizontal line of the 'L' shape were unconnected, so resolute anglers could comfortably walk between the two gravel pits to find their swim.

On this snowy day, my sister Kiera and I had cycled from our nearby village of Eccles, to the pits at Aylesford, for half a day of fishing. We had bread and dough for bait and the enthusiasm of the young and foolish.

The first problem was that the water was frozen over and locating any area of 'swim.' where we could conveniently drop a float and some bait was hard to find. Yet we were not despondent, partly because we were budding chumps, but also because we had a little knowledge. Of course, a little knowledge is a dangerous thing, especially when considering ice and frozen water.

As the older sibling and as the product of my overzealous deliberations with the Encyclopaedia Britannica, I knew that the inhabitants of the Arctic and of Antarctica made holes in the ice and conveniently plopped in their baits. So I set about hacking out a circle of ice to reveal the green water beneath. A rod was tackled up and the first float plopped cheekily into the still crystals that floated within the ring of denser ice. Some thirty minutes later, nothing had happened. We just got colder.

There comes a moment in the day when fishing becomes a pointless activity. Nonetheless, many enthusiasts fail to recognise this watershed. Our motto, purloined from Peter Sabine, our locally celebrated fishing expert, was always, 'if there're fish in there I'll catch 'em'. As a philosophy of optimism, it tilted the scales against the fish; and in our minds elevated we predators, from minnows to marlins, in one move.

Typically with the chumpish behaviour condition, I was already changing the rules, and walking on thin ice; for in the middle of the pit was a huge cluster of plants and wood of island proportions. I made my way cautiously and gingerly across the ice.

Stepping onto 'my island' signified another 'transition;' but this was not the famous Laputa of Gulliver's Travels.

'Kiera! Dry land,' I yelled, and jumped up and down.

My elation or elevation did not last long, and on landing I went straight through the ice and into the freezing water up to my chest. Kiera was useless. She was a frozen icicle, jangling in the wind, stricken with laughter, rhythmically and helplessly hiccupping, on the icy bank.

I first thought I would drown, but spontaneously, a survival instinct came to my rescue, and helped that sad, wet walrus, slither from the water. Laughter? Kiera was still howling on the bank.

'Roach: 1 John: 0'   The fish were safe for another day.

12.   The Caning

During my time at Primary school I got along well with the Head Teacher, Francis Beechgrove and although we were all afraid of him, I loved going out into Aylesford village with our easels, to paint Aylesford's beautiful old Norman Bridge or its charming cottages.

F.A. Beechgrove was a very competent artist and his tableaus graced the school and included some large pictures, which brought a religious theme to our classroom. Mr Beechgrove also loved playing the piano and we pupils learned countless folk songs from all parts of these islands. Occasionally he would expose us to jazz!

Each morning we named the piece of classical music which led us into our assembly. He especially loved Bach, Handel and Delius. Francis also enjoyed playing chess in his office with his pupils and one day it gave me a great boost to be the first pupil to beat him at the game!

Mr Beechgrove also enjoyed gardening and I learned much from him in the school plot, especially how to prune roses and when to mulch around the borders and to spot the difference between a perennial and an annual.

I had never been caned before, but the Head regularly spanked boys, including myself, by pulling us unceremoniously over his knee and lashing us mercilessly with his flattened hand.

During one particular break time, I had been involved in a dispute in the playground with a boy called Lee Wiles. We usually worked things out, but on this occasion we were still arguing when we came into the classroom to take our places for the art lesson.

Lee sat down in front of me but he hadn't finished yet! Still angry, he took four brushes, dipped them in paint and water and then flicked them over my new shirt. A feeling of sheer horror swept over me; not about Lee's outrageous, provocative action; but the predicted response of my mother to my shirt splattered with paint. Idiotically and viscerally, I responded with my own four brush slosher over Lee's grinning face.

All went silent. The bespectacled face of the Head teacher was spotted peering through the lower pane of glass in the classroom door. It was a menacing look, over his glasses, and it chilled us all to the bone. Sensing mischief, in he strode, like a matador, into the arena.

I know it's odd, but why is it, that when something is wrong it gets noticed immediately by those who might mete out punishment? Beechgrove paused and then looked up at his picture of the 'Madonna and Child'. It was covered in blue dots and splodges.

'Who is responsible for this?' he snarled menacingly. Then gesticulating dramatically, in the direction of the picture on the wall, he made his theatrical point.

'What barbarian is responsible for this?'

Now, the game was up, but I was not going to take the 'wrap' for weasel Wiles. No sir! I would wait for the scrape of his chair and the raising of his skinny arm. Moments were frozen in time, and then surprisingly, it happened. We both stood up, each raising a hand.

'Come to my office' snapped Beechgrove.

The carpet pile of the office was soft and deep and kind. It felt like comfortable sand upon the beach. Lee was ahead of me. We stood beside Mr Beechgrove's great multi drawer bureau.

He opened one drawer and withdrew the most exquisite, satin covered book. On its cover, in gold letters, were the words: 'PUNISHMENT BOOK.' He turned away from Lee and addressed me directly.

'I'm surprised at you', he said.

The words had the desired effect. I felt miserable. I had let everyone down.

He placed the precious purple book onto the bureau and opened the first page. Inside, I caught sight of the earliest villains of the school, their names recorded from the late 1800s in a script full of flourish: their names and dates of their offences and the punishments meted out. Beechgrove completed our entries with his elegant Osmiroid pen, carefully pausing to absorb the excess ink with his blotter. My heart sank. I would be among that pantheon of offenders.

'Right, let's get this over with,' said Beechgrove as he opened another drawer and reached again into the bureau. This time Lee and I could see the stash of canes.

Some canes were fat and short, others long; some repaired with tape and others thin and whippy. My mind raced. What kind of cane would inflict the most pain? Thin and whippy? Short and fat?

He picked one out and flexed it as a test; and then replaced it; then chose another more supple and more spiteful looking. Beechgrove was very fussy.

'You first,' he said to Lee, as he seized his right hand and held it out. One, two, three. Left hand, one, two, three! Over in seconds. Lee broke into sobs and held his hands under his armpits.

'Next,' crackled Beechgrove. One, two, three. One, two, three!

The pain was excruciating but I wouldn't cry. Where would I put my hands? What icy water would take away the sting?

We were taken back to the classroom amid mutterings from our classmates. 'What happened?' 'Did you get the cane?' 'Did it hurt?' I wouldn't cry, but I was bitterly upset that I had disappointed myself that day.

By the next morning the cleaner had wiped away the watercolour splashes from the picture. Fortunately the framed glass had protected it, but all was not as it had been.

13.   <u>Won Life</u>

I liked the bible stories as a kid but early on found them mystical yet implausible and even ridiculous at times. For me, Genesis made no sense at all and our school vicar at St Peter's Primary, the Reverend Lowell, a good man and firmly Church of England, insisted on the literal truth of all things biblical. He was always of the conviction that he was right, but in my child eyes, his faith always got in the way of his reasoning.

 I always felt that you could be a good person without being a religious one. At the time, there seemed to be no unbelievers; or only bad people were unbelievers and only good people who went to church or got married at the altar were believers.

My mother's family were Irish Roman Catholics but were 'lapsed' and England's secular society provided no checks and no incentives to modify the acquired behaviour of their adopted country.

I sang in the choir and being adjudged a good reader I chanted out hunks of the bible which I genuinely understood and was even awarded prizes for my knowledge; but what I liked most of all was arguing, and religion gave me ample opportunity to do this.

I irritated the Reverend and I enjoyed that feeling of his awkwardness. I enjoyed the intellectual competition with him, and after all, belief was only veiled opinion. It was the elitism of faith that annoyed me. That faith was accessible but only for the chosen. I did not want to be chosen, only respected for having a different 'take' on it all.

I argued for humility and against human arrogance. Who do we think we are? Do we really think that as a species on this planet, we are really that important in the grand universal scheme? No place for a designer. We are alone so what does it matter that we are alone?

Religious story tellers had been busy creating a fantastical cape to cover our fear of death. Religion existed to cushion our journey at the end of life to our death. Each cultural potter had thrown a pot and called it 'Special' and this carefully crafted creation would allay our fears about the end of life. Why would there be an afterlife? Why should there be an afterlife. Who do we think we are? Are we REALLY that important in this great universe? That makes no sense at all. Death only matters to those who have not yet died.

As a young boy I adored dinosaurs and had hordes of plastic replicas which buoyed up the genuine fossil evidence; the plain logic of it all. Darwin made complete sense and phrases like 'the survival of the fittest', 'adaption' and 'common ancestor' seemed obvious and more brilliant than any magician's trick.

At eighteen, we school students were offered anthropology lessons by a new, young New Zealander, a Mr Halliford. He took us to the Leakeys, Olduvai Gorge, to Pro Consul Africanus; Udabno Pithecus and Zinjanthropus. Wow, what a trip we had! It was so nice to meet Neanderthals and nowadays, the Denisovans. I never lost my passion for the quest. Who are we? Where did we come from? Where are we going?

These wonderful discoveries reinforced my faith in the adaptability and resilience of mankind, so, I developed a really optimistic edge, which suited me nicely; a 'won life mentality' that always made me feel privileged to be on the wonderful planet: to see, hear, taste, smell, touch and reflect on the marvel of its stunning existence and to do the best I possibly could while I was here.

14.   The Cycle Home

The trusty bicycle was the main mode of transport for many men in Eccles village at this time and it was mainly used to take them to their workplace at the paper mills in New Hythe. An early morning procession of men in khaki mackintoshes and flat caps, army style bags and vacuum flasks was a regular sight in the village in the late 50s and early 60s.

However, for boys like myself, in our short grey trousers, our cycles carried us from home in Eccles to school in Aylesford, a distance of under two miles and 'touch wood', my 'Halfords' Pathfinder' bike never let me down.

Indeed, I invested some of my hard earned cash in a milometer which measured the distances I travelled each time the wheels turned. I do remember, on one occasion, travelling speedily past the recreation ground and being asked by my friend Harold Frobisher, who was cycling behind me, where my new milometer was attached. I foolishly stood up on the pedals and indicated with my right toe that it was on the front forks. The toe, followed by the foot, dramatically went into the front spokes and I can clearly recall completing a full cartwheel with the bike landing on top of me a moment later. Ouch!

Harold raced me home most afternoons when school had finished and he inevitably beat me because of his extremely annoying Sturmey Archer three speed gear change on his bike. My 'Pathfinder' with no gears, and slightly smaller tyres at 24inch, could not keep up, however hard I peddled, however hard I puffed and panted.

Harold was irritatingly superior on his sophisticated bike, but also in other things as well. Take for example his archery equipment. I had a fine elm bow and some well crafted, home-made arrows; oh, but Harold had a professionally made bow and professionally made feathered arrows which he fired at least double the distance of my own.

Harold lived in Cork Street, an only son, and worthy of a place among the archers of Crecy or Agincourt, or so we thought.

Riding home one afternoon from Aylesford was different. Not only was I wearing a stylish pair of long trousers, but Harold had thrown down the metaphorical gauntlet and challenged me to another race home. I accepted and we raced through the village, passed 'The Chequers' pub and Dadson's general store towards Friar's corner. We were neck and neck.

I held him on the straight road and being 'neck and neck' I wasted no energy thinking about squashing the legendary stag beetles and the glow worms which were traditionally found on this stretch of road.

We raced on, but Harold started to pull away. Another defeat! Then further disaster! The lower right leg of my long trousers caught in the chain and cog; and within a moment my trousers were torn from foot to crotch in one ripping movement. Disaster turned into farce as I pulled over, while Harold disappeared into the distance like a Tour de France yellow jersey holder.

Disenchanted with racing, and with Harold probably in the next county, I sauntered along on the bike, worrying about the damage to my trousers, the fact that I had no cycle clips and the reception I would receive when I got home, especially from my mother.

I passed the sandpits where a local boy had drowned the previous year, where sand martins nested, the stag beetles trundled and glow worms twinkled at night. I passed the orchards of cherry and apple, passed Westwell's Farm and Loxley's house on the left, up towards the village post office and the Walnut Tree public house. But my eye was distracted and drawn to a small crowd of men in the cornfield beyond the post office. Too good an opportunity to miss! What was going on? An accident?

With my trouser leg flapping, I approached the group and could see that they had been digging in the field and appeared to have created a couple of trenches. Looking for bodies eh? The men were different to the usual people around the village, and although they were digging, one wore a cravat, another a collar and tie, and the other two, chunky knitted jerseys.

'Hi,' I said, 'may I ask what you're looking for?'

The thin faced bespectacled man in the cravat took my question.

'Well', we're doing an archaeological dig because we think there's a Roman villa here in the field.'

'It seems a strange place to live.......in the middle of a field.'

'True,' he replied, 'it would be quite different then.'

'Then?' I replied.

'Yes, well we're thinking about A.D.75; there's a good water supply, the soil is flinty but decent quality and look, here are some bits of the hypocaust; the central heating system.'

He put a red piece of tile into my hand and it glowed; I glowed. Wow!

'I'll see you again. Can I come back?' 'Feel free,' he said.

'You can do some digging next time,' chipped in the man with the tie, with a smile.

I peddled away like a madman. At home I was full of the story. I went to the encyclopaedia and swotted up on Romano British villas; simple things like, what were they? Who lived here in Eccles before us? Did the inhabitants look and feel as I do? Did the archaeologist mean that they were Romans living there, you know, like Julius Caesar, or were they British like Caractacus? What was their family life like? Were they chastised by their mothers for biking disasters?

'What on earth have you done to your new trousers?' yelped my mother. 'Caught in my chain Mum ; I couldn't do anything about it' 'Always got an answer, haven't you?'

Over the ensuing weeks and months I was true to my word and dropped by to chat to the men about the excavations of this Romano British villa. They told me it was inhabited between A.D.79 and A.D.290. They discovered a hypocaust, lots of Kentish rag stone and a yellow mortar floor but most spectacular of all, beneath the floor, they found at least three skeletons. I saw a female skeleton in a foetal position. It was the first 'real life' skeleton I ever saw.

On my final visit before they closed the site, the cravat man showed me what he called, 'votive offerings of bird bones' and an infant burial. A baby! Why had it died so young?

This experience of visiting the excavations after school gave me an enduring interest in archaeology and in the history of this fascinating world I lived in. Additionally, if I wore long trousers on my bike, I always wore cycle clips!

15.   The Knockdown

I got run over one day. Let me tell you how it happened.

My father had bought a nearly new Ford Consul in Newark grey livery, with a slick column change; and with the registration number 580 BKO- if my memory serves me well.

It was a greedy little beggar, guzzling petrol but consuming the miles. Today, the beast had run out of fuel and stood empty tanked in front of the house. With its big smiley radiator and its sad eyed headlights it was already beginning to look forlorn and neglected.

'A car without petrol is like a man without blood.'

We'd had a good fall of snow and the roads were slippery but passable. The journey to the petrol station was a few miles in distance, so we were offered the option: 'Who wants to walk up with me to the service station on Bluebell Hill and who wants to stay at home?'

I smartly stepped forward. Another adventure!

My middle sister, Tessa or TS, as we called her, came along with us and the walking pattern was to be father at the front, TS in the middle and yours truly following up behind.

It was really, really cold and we slogged up Red Cow Lane and turned right at the top of the road. We hacked along the road, parallel to the chalk pit, and made it to the one way section which came out at the bottom of Bluebell Hill below Kits Coty.

It was a brilliant, clear day and the sun shone upon the coverlet of white snow so brightly, that well-defined shadows stood out like embroidered ferns against the whiteness. We had chosen the safety of the banked snow to walk upon and as we trudged, the slinky snake of traffic passed us. For safety we adopted our walking order.

Ahead of us was Maidstone; the sun glittering in the cold, clear air, in a brilliant blue sky. With the security and the safety of a bright day we walked on, first speaking about the death of one of the Black boys from Wouldham, on his motorcycle, not far from the 'Running Horse' pub; and then began chattering about the 'Ghost of Bluebell Hill.' At that time, the story of the ghost of Blue Bell Hill was one of the most popular stories circulating around our villages in the Medway valley.

The story was about unsuspecting motorists who reckoned they saw a woman, running out in front of their car or motorcycle, late at night. The woman often stared into the driver's terrified eyes, before being struck by the victim's vehicle and then vanishing. Traumatised drivers who stopped, never discovered any evidence of a collision, and never found a victim.

The earliest rumour in our village was slightly different and of an unknown woman who died in a tragic car accident in the late 1950s to early 1960s, near the bridge, over the old Chatham Road. According to the rumour mongers, there had been two cars involved in the collision, and three out of the four women in one car tragically died. In one of the cars, one of the women was a bride-to-be, and she was due to be married the following day.

As well as the mythology of a ghost jumping in front of cars, there were schoolmates describing experiences of a female hitch-hiker on Bluebell Hill. Motorists, who pulled over to pick her up, seated her in the rear, only for her to disappear shortly after the vehicle set off. I visualised the horrified motorcyclists who were haunted by the terrifying thought that their pillion passenger had fallen off and was lying somewhere on the dark road!

I started to breathe more heavily as we commenced the slight climb up the slope towards the Cossington Petrol station.

'What do you think about the ghost of Bluebell Hill, Dad?'

He glanced briefly over his shoulder.

'A load of old rubbish; no such things; people just imagine them!'

I could see the petrol station, set in its orange and white colours, about half a mile ahead....

I opened my eyes. Besieged by bushes; black spiky thorns like spiteful hypodermics in my face; splintered creased bark, lined and cracked; grass damp and broken stemmed; dew clinging to plants in globules of water and broken flakes of snow. I closed my eyes.

My back ached. Sharp thorns, under my skin. It burned. I opened my eyes again... petrol station; where? Orange and white. Voices; can't sleep; arms, legs, head, neck; I touched each of these. I looked at the blue sky. A solitary crow wheeled overhead.

'I'm so sorry.. oh...oh...' a woman moaned '....are you alright....the sun...I couldn't see...I couldn't see....the sun....the sun blinded me.'

An elderly woman motorist stood in front of me, crying; her face in her hands. Step father looked terrified for us; he was with T.S. and she seemed to be shaken but moving. He ignored the woman and attended to my sister. He was shaken and angry with the hysterical motorist. He then related to her that TS and I had been thrown high into the air by her vehicle, causing us to somersault several times and end up in the bushes.

'Luckily they've not been killed'

'I'm sorry, I'm so sorry,' the elderly woman echoed.

She stared into my stepfather's terrified eyes, and appeared so dishevelled, that she looked like she had been struck with a car herself. She wiped her eyes with the back of her hand.

'Are you sure you're alright? Are you sure?'

She reached into her coat pocket. 'Here are my details. What are your details?' They exchanged the information. The woman vanished into her car and drove off towards the sun.

Shortly afterwards we were underway and we trundled on to the Cossington petrol station where we related our story and where the kind petrol station manager made us a cup of tea made with Fussells milk.

'It's not the first time that has happened,' he remarked, 'and it won't be the last.'

16.   The Void

When most of the human race considers the expression, 'The Void,' it is revealed as that massively empty space, that chasm or abyss or lacuna, which comes to mind. But we were no blank, hole, pit or hiatus. Indeed, the existence of voids like us is significant in providing physical evidence for our dark energy. We were a bunch of musicians.

The Void's members at that moment in 1964 were Melvin, Gerry, Rich and Kevin. The problem for the band concerned Melvin's voice, which had 'broken' badly and sounded like the proverbial croaking frog. That's how I got involved; as the possible substitute for Melvin, but of course, there would have to be an audition.

Now, in prehistory, auditions were unheard of, especially for a little band of villagers. Nonetheless, the audition took place at Aylesford Working Men's club with a couple of songs which conspired to show off the vocal range. Melvin had stayed away but the other three, all friends of mine, had hyped it all up until I felt nervous.

Kevin sat behind his drums; Rich hitched his rhythm guitar up to his Selmer amplifier and Gerry 'jammed' away at his sky blue lead guitar.

'Try 'Louie, Louie, by the Kinsmen,' warbled Gerry. Well he would, he wasn't doing the singing and had the benefit of endless rehearsals, but feeling positive, and leading from the front suited me. I was self-centred and already reasonably self obsessed.

'In the Midnight Hour,' a Wilson Picket number went well enough, even while I waited for the midnight hour. Chuck Berry's 'Around and Around,' followed, and my closeted world did go around and around, and it surprised me how it sounded so reasonably near the original.

'That's great,' said band leader Gerry. 'I want you to learn the Stones, 'The Last Time ,' and The Animals, ' House of the Rising Sun.' 'You've got the gig.'

Over the weeks the three originals rehearsed every Thursday and the band learned 'Booker T and the MGs 'Green Onions.' We moved on to Eccles Working Man's Club where I learned 'The Last Time,' 'Don't Think Twice It's Alright, ' 'Memphis,' ' Roll over Beethoven,' ' Jonny Be Good,' ' Time is on my Side' 'Route 66' 'Everybody needs Somebody to Love,' and 'Heart full of Soul' and so on and on. We were 'The Void' and we had a heart full of soul.

We rehearsed next door to the bar at the working man's club and it was quite an experience. Teddy boys in winkle pickers, rockers in quiffs, sideburns, greasy slicked back hair, sharp pointy noses and chins jutting out in defiance of the established order.

Our rehearsals became more fraught, not musically, but socially, as fights erupted next door in the social club. We really wanted to make music but the neighbours were both disruptive and scary. One spiv poked his head in the door.

 'Oi mate, can you play any Lonnie Donegan or Elvis? How about Blue Suede Shoes?'

Others, alcohol drenched, followed, and the thought of ever playing there amid the latent hostility and anger caused us to look somewhere else, firstly at Burham Primary School Hall, beside 'The Windmill' and I travelled in from our Strood home, then.....

Gerry: 'We've booked 'The Royal Albert Hall'

Me: 'The Royal Albert Hall, London?'

Gerry: 'The 'Royal Albert' pub in Burham; it has a side hall attached.

After all, we were 'The Void,' full of dark energy.

17.   I Rescued Shelley Too

Alas! This Is Not What I Thought Life Was

Alas! This is not what I thought life was.
I knew that there were crimes and evil men,
Misery and hate; nor did I hope to pass
Untouched by suffering, through the rugged glen.
In mine own heart I saw as in a glass
The hearts of others ... And when
I went among my kind, with triple brass
Of calm endurance my weak breast I armed,
To bear scorn, fear, and hate, a woeful mass!

Percy Bysshe Shelley

On the sticky edge of the mighty Medway River there is a slippery promontory which juts out into the water and which is continually battered and restored by the merciless currents of that feisty-flowing, fulminated, mercurial water. On the quiet curve behind the jutting elbow, all manner of artefacts wash onto the shore over time.

One day I found a fine clay pipe blackened through use and with a hole in its bowl. I closed my eyes and imagined the bewhiskered boatman tired of puffing ineffectually on his pipe and casting it into the creamy waters in frustration or disgust. On another occasion, at low tide, along the shoreline, I discovered some chunky bottles with unusual glass stoppers; but on a third visit let me tell you what I found.

I had been alone, investigating an old WWII air raid shelter, looking for clues, and as I emerged, my eyes were hastily adjusting to the light; and were drawn across the river, towards the C.A.V. and Blaw Knox engineering works.

Out of the corner of my eye I saw a dumper lorry approach the open ground some half a mile ahead of me. To my astonishment the tipper, lifted up its scoop and dumped a huge amount of refuse. Presumably it was 'in fill,' and dumped for the official purpose of reclaiming the slowly eroding river's edge.

Let me tell you now, that at fourteen, I was outraged at the sheer hooliganism of the authorities. Alas! This is not what I thought life was. Dumping waste, fouling up the river's foreshore; it was surely a criminal act, a monstrosity.

Curiously the refuse attracted no gulls to scavenge and skirmish over the spoils, none to cluster round and scrimmage and ruck like ill tempered rugby players. Oddly these sentinels of sky and shoreline had gone missing.

In a cobalt plume of blue smoke and with a feral roar the lorry sped off, churning up the soft, richly dark earth of the old shore as it went on its way. The driver, unperturbed, provocatively flashed his lights and beeped his horn. He didn't care.

I walked slowly towards the distant pile of waste trying to work out exactly what it was. Slowly, with each step it dawned on me. The pieces of waste gradually took shape, like a giant jigsaw puzzle. Dark colours. Light edges? Wooden blocks? Bricks? Books!

The lorry had dumped hundreds of books. Hundreds of old books as landfill. I stooped over and picked a faded, maroon covered 827 page tome of Lord Byron's, 'Poetical Works, ' and inside the damning truth, 'Withdrawn from ......Public Library.'

Books! I couldn't step on them. I wouldn't stand on them; although with their piled height I could have climbed and climbed and planted my flag. Sure the gulls would not be interested. But I was interested.

I ran home to Sycamore Road as quick as quick.

'What's wrong? What's wrong?' yelped my mother.

'Books,' I gasped between breaths. 'Loads of them....dumped books.'

'What are you going to do?'

'Books Mum; I'm going to get them. I can't believe it. Can you believe it; they've dumped books...hundreds of them? What the hell are they thinking dumping books?'

I ran through the house out into the shed and returned with the garden wheelbarrow. Ignoring some odd glances from motorists on the main road, I crossed over the railway line on my way to the river side and quickly arrived at the massive mountain of books. No, the pile was not a Mount Everest or a Kilimanjaro or even a Ben Nevis; and rocks aren't books but imagine, 'big'. So, what would I take? What would you take?

Into my wheelbarrow I stacked and squeezed Byron, Tennyson, Coleridge, Blake, Bronte, Eliot, Twain, Longfellow, Dickens, and dozens of other good men and women. In my mind I had excited them all at the prospect of a new home. I struggled to my house, chatting to them as I went, reassuring them that they were going to a good place.

'Now Mr Dickens, you'll feel right at home. See there's Rochester Castle over the river. Remember?'

Next, I set out on a second rescue journey with the barrow.

This time I piled Melville onto Alcott, Dumas on Machiavelli, Ruskin onto Cervantes, Fenimore Cooper onto Goethe and millions more on millions more. I felt like I'd been on the battlefield rescuing friends. Oh, and while I remember, I rescued Shelley too.

18. <u>Bligh Way, My Way</u>

In 1963 we moved from Eccles to Strood and that seismic schism had repercussions which echoed on and on and on.

It was at that address that my red haired, feisty mother issued her 'Declaration for Working Boys' when she said: 'Go out now and don't come home until you've got yourself a part-time job.'

Mercifully I found Jack and Deborah Cranford, a childless couple from Aylesbury, who owned H & G News Agency in Darnley Road and who I persuaded to offer me a small paper round for 7s and 6d a week.

I had many good times at the shop and the couple took me under their wings; on two occasions taking me to the Newsagents' Dinner and paying for me to hire a dinner jacket and dickey bow tie; and on another bringing me a fine brown suede tie as a present from Majorca. They even sold me a small oak cabinet and a noble, brass embossed, oak box, which I keep beside my bed today.

One morning after having 'marked up' the papers, it turned out that the paper boy for Bligh Way had failed to arrive for the round. It was a couple of extra shillings for me to do the circuit and so off I went.

I biked up to the start of Bligh Way and got cracking with the heavy bag of papers. As I folded one of the dull dailies, I caught the silhouette of an old guy leaning against the roadside lamp post. He was dressed for work in a beige mackintosh and one of the old fashioned, army style khaki bags over his shoulder, with its ubiquitous protruding vacuum flask; his flat cap pulled down over his forehead.

I think opticians call it 'peripheral' and it's the part of our sight, right at the edge of our field of vision. Well my eyes caught this old fellah, falling forward, into the road.

You know when we fall, instinct compels us to throw out our arms to prevent damage and protect ourselves, but he did nothing of the sort. He lurched forward, like a felled pine, and collapsed full face first onto the concrete road. For me the shock of his involuntary fall, where his face hit concrete was truly appalling to my senses.

I rushed across and had turned him over in an instant; comforting him with a few words and tucking my news bag underneath his cap less head. I looked round and caught sight of a young man hurrying by.

'Can you help? We need to 'phone an ambulance.'

'Sorry mate, I'm in a rush, I'm late for work,' he replied, and was gone.

The old man beside me did not look good. Blood oozed from his mouth, his teeth were smashed and he was not responding. My dilemma was whether to leave the injured man to run to the 'phone box and call 999 or hang on with him. Incredibly, a man pulled up in a car, miraculously jumped out and said he would call the ambulance.

I hung around until the ambulance came. I felt that this stranger was somehow my responsibility and I would not fail him. People passed by, looked on, and grimaced. A small crowd gathered. The ambulance driver took me aside,

'Don't worry son,' he said, 'you did all you could. He probably had a massive heart attack and was dead before he hit the road.'

I went on with the delivery of my papers and kept thinking of the dead man. I felt hollow.

'Headline: Dead Man! Newspaper Boy Questioned!'

I explained what had happened to Mr and Mrs Cranford and they advised me to, 'try not to dwell on it.'

She turned to her husband. 'A cuppa corfee, Mr Cranford?'

I cycled home, up Cedar Road, across to Hawthorne Road, out of the traffic onto the pavement; alone with my thoughts. Halfway along Hawthorn, a police car slowed and the driver wound down his window and called over: 'Perhaps when you're old enough sonny, you'll be able to ride on the road.' I said nothing and bumped down the kerb onto the road.

I arrived at home and got changed for school. My grandmother said, 'don't let it get in at you.'

I cycled to the train station at Cuxton, caught the train to Maidstone and then the trolley bus to Oakwood Park to school, but however far I travelled, the memory of my first contact with death never left me.

P.S. About a fortnight later a letter arrived at the news agency thanking the paperboy:

' .....who helped my father that day.'

19.   <u>Always Say 'Hello!'</u>

At the toss of an old penny coin, Jack Yorkson and I decided to go our separate ways, as we hitchhiked back through France with a planned rendezvous in two days time, beneath the coloured clock tower in Calais.

 The year was 1968 and we were returning home at the end of a 2000 mile hitchhiking journey around Europe. Experience had taught us that being together would mean a famine of lifts for both of us; and we were two, very keen young men, eager to return to England.

The tossed coin, spun around and landed in Jack's favour. Off he went and as fate would have it, we would not meet again in France but in his home village of Charing, Kent.

Being alone had never bothered me too much and I steadily and resolutely made my way towards Paris. I walked for miles, feasting on a bread roll and a can of sweet Coca Cola.

I carried my rucksack, tent and sleeping bag and wore my Italian straw hat- which was very seasonal for Italy- but not suitable for the incoming and unpleasant French weather.

 The hitch hiking lifts were intermittent and after many hours travel and the suburbs' steady descent into darkness, a driver eventually dropped me into the heart of the city.

Paris is a beautiful place, but it loses its allure when a visitor is penniless, without food and without refreshment. I found myself alongside the River Seine, tired, disconnected from the patrons of the cafes and craving sleep.

Alongside the river, was a beautifully maintained pathway and intermittently, on the pathway, semi circular arches were set into the wall, with a series flat seating or resting places.

Needing no encouragement I unrolled my sleeping bag onto the flat stone resting place, climbed inside and used my tent as a pillow. I slept solidly and woke around five a.m., looked around and admired the serene, misty river for a few moments.

I left my stone bed behind and headed out onto the streets, quickly finding a bench on which to pause for a few moments to review my options. I watched water bubble up from the drains to cleanse away the gutter detritus of the previous day. Great idea, I thought.

A girl crossed the empty street and sat beside me but at the far end of the bench; she was about my age but looked tired and careworn. Her make-up was smudged and like me she had signs that she had 'slept in the clothes she stood up in.' She didn't speak and neither did I, but together for a moment, we watched the cleansing water coursing its way along the Parisian gutter.

I stood up, gathered my belongings and walked away. Maybe I should have said, 'bonjour....' but my options for the day ahead buzzed around my mind. I rambled onwards while considering my limited choices. Conclusion: Keep walking!

I walked and walked and walked. Such a colossus of a city! It was then that I spotted an opportunity to approach the auto route heading north and perhaps pick up a driver heading for the channel port. Another great idea! So with a spring in my step and a hunger in my belly, I walked to a convenient spot on the slip road and stuck out my lucky thumb. Almost immediately I hauled in a driver ready to help.

Actually, I must be honest here and say, that it was in fact a police car with the word 'Gendarmerie' written all over it. What would I say? How should I play this? Should I run? Then as the gendarme climbed out of the vehicle the answer came: When in doubt act it out. They fell for the dodgy hunchback of Notre Dame and they would fall for the slightly mad, badly French speaking bogtrotter with his fake Irish brogue.

The gendarmes approached me, shaking their heads and speaking fantastic French phrases, some of which I had never heard before, even on our Whitfield French course at school. To sum it up, they were not happy that I was about to enter a motorway on foot, and indicated that I would not keep up with other motorway traffic and that I should immediately get into their squad car, presumably to spend some more time in their company at their clubhouse or AKA the police station.

We hurried along the motorway for some distance; the two officers chatting to each other and ignoring the chump on the back seat. Spits and spots of rain began to fall and the car wipers began their monotonous rhythm. How far was the police station? How long would I be delayed? Then abruptly we stopped, and they directed me to climb out.

'That direction' and he pointed. 'Calais', he added.

I nodded and nodded; that's always convincing; but to be fair to them, I was on my way, on the edge of the city heading north towards my rendezvous. All hail the Gendarmerie!

I began walking again in the steady rain and apart from the occasional stop to compose myself I walked for the whole day and into the evening.

Just before darkness fell, I drank deeply from a roadside water fountain and it quenched my urgent thirst. I would have to manage. I had left the suburbs behind and was now well into the French countryside. My Italian straw hat had been a veritable boon in the Florentine sun but in the northern rain it came to resemble partly cooked pasta. Oh that I could have eaten my hat!

I walked on into the darkness, into the rain, with the gurgle of water bubbling along the road's edge and sloshing and swishing around my head. Here and there, on the road, were farm cottages shrouded by the late summer darkness with the merest hint of slanted rainy light coming through each window. I walked on. The cottages disappeared and I found myself in the middle of a place I called 'nowhere.' Huge trees overhung the road edges; cars had vanished and still the rain fell and the wind stirred.

My stomach rumbled and my throat was again becoming parched. I stuck out my tongue to catch droplets. Where would I sleep? The problem nagged at me like an aching tooth. Teeth! Such a nuisance! My mind burned and dimmed and tired. Today is gone. Whatever had to be done would wait until tomorrow. Tomorrow I would begin again. Start from here, make a plan, and execute the plan. Execute! Madame Guillotine! I could sleep anywhere.

Up ahead through the dark and rain I could see the dim, indistinct outline of a railway bridge and suddenly the bridge became my house. I love bridges and I don't know why. I just love them. Any old bridge will do or any new bridge too. It doesn't have to be the Ponte Vecchio or the Forth Road Bridge. This bridge would be special for it would provide a roof over my head for the night. As I got closer I could see it more distinctly through the misty rain.

I also noticed the outline of a standing figure just about in the middle of the bridge span and obviously sheltering beneath its arch. I was not alarmed, neither did I feel any fear and as I approached I noticed that the male figure wore a massive forest-green, great coat with its collar turned up. On his feet were heavy old fashioned boots, while on his head was a bag like cap, again in heavy material like the coat. His face was turned away, not even in silhouette, so it was difficult to see his features, but one thing I did notice was the bowl end of a pipe in his mouth.

I turned away and began to remove my rucksack and tent and sleeping bag and in that instant I felt the strong desire to speak to the man; to say ' hello....bonjour!' at least, mainly for the uniqueness of the two of us being thrown together beneath this bridge.

It never occurred to me that it was odd. Here we were, two people, sheltering under the same bridge in the middle of nowhere. Say hello! I thought. Always say hello!

I turned back to face the man, ready to say 'bonjour or hello!' but he was gone. But where? It was surely impossible, in the instant I turned away, for the man to make off and disappear into the ether. Simply not possible!

I hurried along to the end of the bridge and checked the steep slope up to the railway lines. Impossible! I hurried back and inspected the other end of the embankment and the steep climb was impossible. The road was clear in both directions.. he had vanished.

Chronically tired, I wrapped myself in my sleeping bag and tent and fell asleep. I heard no trains in the night and in the morning I could find no footprints of the stranger on the muddy ground. Who or what was he? I would never know.

Getting myself together on a new sunny day, I stood out on the road and hung out my lucky thumb. Literally within ten minutes an empty coach pulled up. Unreal!

'Calais?' said the driver. 'Calais, yes!'

The kind driver dropped me beneath the coloured clock in Calais, but Jack Yorkson had already been there and was now safely home. It took another day before I knocked on our door at Syracuse Road and another twenty four hours to reflect on the night before, under the bridge.

20. <u>The Open Book</u>

This story about my Aunty Maeve started in Ireland, or to be more precise, in that huge house located 'in a dip' in County Mayo. When I picked it over, I could garner very little of her early life at that time and only snippets of information; out of focus black and white photographs and the odd remembered remark were all that remained.

'Ah she was bright, alright, especially at arithmetic.'

Maeve was studious, clever and seemed to have a natural ability to learn most things easily. She loved reading, especially the quests and trials of ancient Irish heroes. Her hand writing was expressive and fancy and frilly. She felt safe at school.

'Ah Maeve, come in, come in, you are doing very well. ' The dark haired, dark eyed girl, responded with a wide grin. She was happy and comfortable with the nuns and always the committed Roman Catholic.

Of her childhood little is now known; the pleasures and pains of her life have long since dissipated, ricocheting around the atoms of the universe, sucked into the vortex and absorbed. Changed!

It was unrecognised in the family that the youngest daughter of Michael Quinn and Mollie Rose McGowan, youthful Maeve, was unsettled, unhappy, becoming increasingly secretive and afraid. How could close family members miss the signs? Why were the signs not recognised?

One answer might be because her mother and sister were also drowning in the same Mayo mud; another might be that it was because her desperate mother was worn to particles on her father's grinding quern of life.

Eventually mother and eldest daughter took the decision to run away to England. They had already moved from New York to Mayo and flight seemed to be their only answer but now, at the cost of leaving young Maeve Quinn behind to face the storm, the two took the same decision.

Maeve's mother and sister always justified their actions by saying that she was too young at thirteen to be taken from school or from Ireland. Her older sister Philomena was seventeen, old enough to work and ready to go to England where she might begin a new life with her mother. The younger daughter could follow when she was old enough to work.

 We will never know how hard it was on Maeve to be left behind... abandoned and at the mercy of a vengeful and brutal father. I know that on one occasion she ran away and hid in a nunnery to escape her father, and the letter I read from a priest spoke ominously of her circumstances. Whether leaving Maeve behind was an act of selfishness and cruelty or common sense and reality we will never know.

Admirably, when she was old enough to escape, she did escape and Maeve arrived in England to join her mother and sister. I remember when I first met her; she had shiny black hair, very white skin and a soft Irish voice. She eventually married Ferdinand Williams or Uncle Ferdy as we called him.

Uncle Ferdy had been an orphan, reared by the great 'Barnardo' organisation. He was witty, clever and worked in the cement works laboratory, testing the quality of the cement. He was a wizard at draughts but would never play chess. I remember him telling his eldest son to, 'eat your brrrrread, Connor', where he rolled his tongue in the funniest way possible.

Perhaps the damage had already been done to Maeve, for even the noise of a washing machine irritated her so much that she had to retreat to the bedroom to lie down and recover. Sadly, her problems with 'her nerves' became a regular feature of Maeve's life to the point where some in my own family said that the attitude of her husband, Ferdy, made her even worse.

The sisters, Philomena and Maeve never seemed close and only infrequently got together; their respective husbands were always wary of each other; and Maeve, Ferdy, Connor and Niall's move from Hillside Crescent and eventual emigration to Australia, meant they would see even less of each other.

On the surface it seemed that the move, as iconic £10.00 migrants, would surely help Maeve in the more relaxed and sunny climes of Australia. The boys and Ferdy would flourish and fortunes would be made. Nice idea!

'The best laid plans of mice and men,' would be undone and unravelled. It would not work out like that, as Maeve's condition worsened, her stress levels increased, and the medical expenses mounted. The families exchanged letters and cards of course, but distance is a playground bully making life difficult even unbearable. Eventually they returned from Australia; with their life plan needing a rethink; to continue with their previous life, but this time in Aylesford, along from the railway station.

I knocked at the door and my Aunty Maeve answered it with a nervous smile. She never troubled me with an explanation of her feelings. Aunty Maeve, Grandmother, Mollie Rose McGowan and my own mother, Philomena, were never 'open books.' Secrecy was part of their survival pack.

'Ah John, come in now. Can I get you a cup of tea?' Aunty Maeve asked.

We spoke about my parents, about school, my grandmother, about Aylesford and the journey on my blue Suzuki motorcycle EKN 32C!

'Would you want a biscuit? So you came over to visit me?' she enquired.

'Yes, I'm taking my 'O' levels' I paused, 'If it's alright, I'll try and stop by to see you over the next few weeks,' and I kept my promise, visiting her three or four times in all. We keep our promises. My liking for her grew over the visits and I loved her soft, Irish voice; her sheer kindness and biscuits!

 Months elapsed and my poor exam results came through but we all live to fight another day! Christmas passed and with the New Year came the news: Aunty Maeve had taken an overdose of tablets; she left her Aylesford house and walked to the Carmelite Friary on the edge of the village towards Eccles. She was alone, beyond desperate, but feeling safe in that religious place.

By the time Maeve arrived at the Friars, the medicinal overdose was well and truly into her system. She collapsed and was helped by the monks; rushed to hospital where tragically she died. Maeve left behind a grieving husband and two sons; a sister, mother, nieces, nephews and questions.

The funeral at Aylesford cemetery was the first and worst I ever attended. Both families were shattered, bewildered, looking for answers. I witnessed her coffin move in the limousine as the rear doors were opened; she shuddered and moved. Suicide was appalling especially for those who were left behind. It brought me a profound sense of failure. My earlier visits to see her now seemed shrivelled and pointless. I could not see them for what they were. I cried and cried in pain.

We buried Aunty Maeve under a cherry tree with a headstone showing an 'open book' with Maeve's life and death simply summarised on the left hand 'page.'

Our family tree started to splinter on that day, over the sandwiches, back at Aunty Maeve's house in Aylesford. It was not Aunty Maeve's 'fault'; somehow she was a victim of negligence, carelessness; had we lost her because we were selfish and self obsessed? Someone was guilty; someone had not done enough; another had done too much. Someone would be drawn and quartered!

The family tree struck by emotional lightning split asunder and fell silently, with uncanny stealth, into the darkness and loneliness of life's forest. There was no argument, no blood, just resentment and blame and a quiet darkness. All were broody. Maeve's sons were abandoned at the critical time when they needed support.

I had not seen Uncle Ferdy at all, but I visited Aunty Maeve's grave regularly and always cried. In my last year at school, I noticed a small first year boy instantly recognisable as Connor, Maeve's eldest son. We spoke briefly to each other.

Decades elapsed and my grandmother and mother always claimed that Uncle Ferdy had taken his sons back to Australia. Grandmother passed away. I accepted the reality of the funeral day; but above all I accepted this Australia explanation without as much as a murmur. That was lazy of me I admit, but I continued to visit the grave a couple of times a year to place a wreath, to shed a tear and still wonder why.

In 2010 I walked across to Aunty Maeve's grave with some flowers but the sweet cherry blossom tree had been cut down and from the distance the headstone looked odd. The right side of the stone appeared to have graffiti over its surface, and yet.........astonishingly the right hand side of 'the open book' had been filled with someone's written details. Uncle Ferdy had died. The myth that he was in Australia was exposed.

I was shocked. I walked round and round in a trance. I found a pen and copied down the details. Later that day I contacted the Local Authority and found that Uncle Ferdy had been living locally with his second wife and on that day I discovered Connor and Niall's whereabouts. Here is the first email from my long lost cousin.. I hope you like it as much as I did!

Dear John,

What GREAT news, after 43 years, to hear that your cousin is looking for you! I do have visual memories of you and your parents and three sisters all those years ago. I have also wondered over the years where you all were, and what your lives were like? We have a HUGE amount of catching up to do, but before we do, I just wanted to make sure that I have the correct email address? My stepmother Mable is not great when it comes to computers and makes very little contact with us in Australia. I only received your contact details this morning by email via my mother in law Monica, who is a very good communicator and is in contact with us down here in Australia every week.

I look forward to hearing from you soon. I also have a hotmail address, just in case you have problems with my Outlook address. I tend to use xxx most of the time. In reserve I use xxx as back up !

Has Niall been in touch with you? If he had not mentioned about our Mum's headstone needing renovating and us putting Dad's details on the other side of the open book you would not have found us? They say that life moves in mysterious ways and it is bizarre that it takes the death of our father to rekindle our long lost and awaited contact with our family on Mum's side. As you are probably aware Dad was adopted and had no known blood family. So you and your family are our only known blood relatives. Thank you so very much for making this contact and before I ramble on, I had better send this to make sure it goes to you John. I must say your email address intrigues me! I look forward to hearing from you as soon as possible. All my love,

Connor x

21. Better than Golf

On Wednesday afternoons at the age of eighteen my good friend Jack Yorkson and I were offered a fascinating choice at our school: To join the golf playing school fraternity, or to visit the local hospital to assist people suffering from psychological problems.

For both of us the choice was simple. Whether I was influenced by my earlier experience with my aunt's psychological challenges, or with Mr Field next door in Eccles, I'll never really know, but we embraced the chance with youthful vigour and some trepidation. For me it represented an opportunity to glimpse into an unknown, mysterious world, which when mentioned at school our choice of menu was peppered with bad jokes. Truthfully Jack and I, were afraid.

On our first visit to the grey castle-like buildings of Barming, we were taken into a seemingly parallel world. It looked uncannily like a prison and it didn't help that 'Barming' sounded very like 'barmy' which meant 'mad' in the parlance of the day.

We were 'out of our comfort zone' and this was an understatement. We were uncertain, afraid and inadequate. A visit to Bedlam was just what the shrinks ordered and better than golf by a padded cell.

A nurse introduced us to some patients. Firstly we met Peter, a tall dark haired young man, around fifteen years old. Here he was in this totally adult environment standing in front of a wall and rocking himself forwards and backwards, often deliberately banging his head.

The nurse interrupted our thoughts.

'If you ask him, he can tell you all the bus arrival and departure times across the county. Ask him what the times are for the Number 7 or Number 33 to Tonbridge.' The boy rhythmically ebbed like the waves up against a sea wall. I spoke, but he ignored my voice. He was in a boat, far out to sea.

We asked him about the buses. The nurse was right. Sadly Peter did know.

'And this is Mr Angley,' she said, pointing towards an elderly untidy looking man, who 'on cue' deftly performed a discrete glissando at the piano.

'He had a breakdown after his wife died.'

The nurse cupped her hand to conceal her whispered secret:

'He wanted his wife's wedding and engagement rings but they would not budge, so he cut each of her fingers off to remove them.' If she wanted to shock us, she succeeded.

'And here we have Matt,' she said. 'Matt likes to play chess, don't you Matt?'

Matt was a very grey faced twenty something. He looked disinterested and resigned. He did not speak. Behind her hand she again whispered, 'he's very religious. Do either of you play?' Jack looked across at me and I responded.

'I play a little but as an atheist! Will I do? Does he want someone to play him each week?'

'That would be great. Now come along and I'll show you the workshop.'

The workshop was busy. Very busy. Patients were enjoying creating wooden objects and in doing so, making a lot of noise with their mallets and hammers.

Jack and I stood limply by, as the nurse described the activity and the objects being made by the patients. Wooden trays, egg containers, stools, boxes and such like.

So why was one individual looking at me so menacingly and why was that self same individual engaged in bashing his mallet upon the bench and then into his cupped hand, while looking me directly in the eye? Yes, he wishes it was my head, I thought. Jack had reached a similar conclusion.

We both began to circle anti clockwise around the bench and weirdly the patient detected this and started to move round after us. It was all in his eyes. Weird! Piercing! Chilling! Disturbing! Sinister!

In the merry-go-round of life Jack and I were in the front line. We could see the headlines:

'Sixth Form boys bashed up with a mallet,' and this guy with the crazy eyes, looked to mean business.

What good was our brotherly tryst forged in the wilds of Charing now?

'Beauty is truth, truth is beauty, that is all ye know on earth, and all ye need to know'. Time to leg it? That's the truth and that's all you need to know!

With immaculate timing the nurse whisked us off. She turned to us both. 'You looked spooked? Was it Luther?' She giggled. 'He always does that to newcomers.'

'Has he actually harmed anyone?' enquired Jack.

The nurse smiled sympathetically and was about to say something but thought again and refrained.

We came back to the hospital each Wednesday for many weeks and on one of those visits I got to know Matt much better.

We always sat down together and when laying out our chess pieces, I always asked him how he was feeling. I had been told by one of the nurses, that Matt had suffered a mental breakdown at his university lodgings. He had left his home in nearby Ryarsh for University, but sadly had suffered from depression, to such an extent that he took to his bed, sealed the doors and windows and turned the water taps on.

His housemates only realised what had happened when water came seeping through the ceiling and when his door was forced open, it spilled water down the stairs in a torrent.

Matt went home and eventually he found his way to the hospital and into psychiatric care. Matt's tragic story vividly illustrated the condition of depression, a little understood menace that we school students knew little about.

Matt was a good chess player and took some holding, but on this occasion in our game, he had made an elementary error by moving a bishop in the direct path of my queen. He had set no trap and nothing could be gained with the needless sacrifice of his bishop to my voracious queen.

'Are you sure you want to make that move, Matt?' I queried.

He looked at me unflinchingly, in the eye.

'You don't know who I am, do you? Have I been with you so long, and you still do not know me?'

He unsettled me. He spooked me. He leaned across the chess board and then began to rebuke me.

'You are a stumbling block to me; for you are not setting your mind on God's interests, but Man's.' He paused.

'You still do not know who I am!'

'Who do you think you are?' I responded.

'I am Jesus Christ, the Son of the living God, who created the heavens and the earth, a light which cannot be hid in darkness.'

I was confused. I needed an answer; one which did not draw me into his thinking.

'Your move is not a good one, Matt.' I turned to Jack. 'Tell Matt it's not a good move.' Jack smiled and did not provoke him.

'Time to move on,' I think.

On the final session with the patients we arrived at the hospital as usual, and as usual, we circulated among them all, speaking about this and that. Matt was reading, Peter was swaying in the corner of the room and Mr Angley was asleep.

The nurse met us as we entered. 'We have a new patient who has arrived today. He's a chemist. If you want to speak with him, you can. He's interesting and clever.'

The bearded man lay upon his bed, distracted and far away in his thoughts, staring at the ceiling, humming quietly to himself. He needed no company.

Jack and I moved out of the ward and into the main room, to listen to Mr Angley, who had just woken and was keen to play for us. Off he went with a rendition of the old First World War song and it surely was a long way to Tipperary from Barming; from school; it was a long way to go- even for the sweetest girl-I might know.

We relaxed into our arm chairs to listen to Mr Angley's impromptu concert. I looked across at my friend Jack. He smiled and nodded in quiet pleasure.

'This is better than golf,' I declared.

'Better than golf' he repeated. Jack paused. A commotion from next door had roused us all.

We ran into the next door ward. The bearded chemist had found the exit door and had made his escape. We rushed to the window to see him sprinting across a ploughed field pursued by three male nurses. One nurse rugby-tackled him and pulled him down. The other two picked him up and helped him back. Soon he was cleaned up, put into his bed and sedated.

'It is better than golf,' mused Jack. 'Yes better than golf', I echoed.

Angley was at the piano midway through his song.

'...and my heart's right there,' chimed in Mr Angley. I turned around and swear I saw a glint in his eye.

22. The Imposter

On one of my summer holidays I contacted a farm in the village of
Goudhurst in Kent, to arrange some apple picking on behalf of myself
and my good friend Tom.

The two of us had roomed together one year during teacher training
and we had shared a long since demolished house at 234 Uttoxeter
Road, Derby.

Tom stood over six feet tall with a shock of ginger hair and although
a smoker and a drinker, his youth and strength ensured his fitness.
He was an accomplished runner and football player. Tom was an ideal
and trusted partner to pick Kentish apples and with our labour, to
make a sack full of money for us both!

Tom came down from Dodworth, a Yorkshire mining village and soon
we were, cosily ensconced on the bus, making our way across to the
pretty Kentish farming village of Goudhurst. We chattered about
our shared past, our friends and our futures. I rambled on about
scrumping apples as a youngster and how we still had hop fields full
of Londoners taking working holidays with their families.

On arrival at the field, we were directed to the orchards and taking
our time, we sauntered along the dirt track, until we stood before
the impressive green lines of apple trees. To the right of the trees
were a few tents where ragged groups of pickers quietly went about
their work.

In front of the trees stood a tractor and on the tractor sat the
farmer, a slightly built, hawk-faced man.

'Right' he screeched, 'have you two picked apples before?'.

Tom shook his head.

'I've done some picking before,' I replied.

'O.K.,' he said, his brown glittering eyes penetrating the ground at our feet. 'Well, you see the ladder beneath that tree? Just pick it up and put it into the tree ready for picking.' He shuddered in his shoulders, and his upper body twitched like a tethered hawk adjusting its feathers.

I'd seen ladders like this before. It was a traditional fruit picking variety with splayed legs for greater stability and at least twelve feet in length. To a seasoned picker, it was possible to stand on the bottom rung and pull it up; but for a novice like me, it was a struggle and clumsily I crashed it onto the outside of the tree. Some plump Bramley apples tumbled down and bounced like green skulls upon the ground, beneath the leafy canopy. My own skull might as well have been among them!

The farmer screeched again and with a squawk he jumped down from his seat.

'You may have picked before, but you've never used a ladder.'

I said nothing. 'Perhaps you picked from dwarf trees, eh?' I didn't answer. 'Perhaps you picked hops, not apples, mate?' I was silent. I was not his 'mate.'

'Now watch,' instructed the farmer, and he carefully lifted the ladder, which was ideally suited for harvesting from taller trees. Very gently, he eased the ladder between the branches like a magician hiding a marked card. 'See, no waste! No apples on the ground!' We were thankful for our lesson!

'You can start straight away. We've an orchard to shift. Go up to Doug and get a couple of collection bags. Alright?'

He hovered above us on the tractor.

'When you've filled them, take the apples to the pallet. There are a couple of ladders here, so you can start on this row.'

That day we worked until darkness fell in shards of jet through the trees. Worryingly I began to wonder if Tom hated heights and that was why he was reluctant to climb into the upper branches. Instead he chose to leave the highest apples dangling on the trees like Christmas baubles. Nah! That can't be true. We had already formed a partnership; ready to split the proceeds of our labour, and yet I had a hunch that perhaps I would be spending most of my time among the twigs and sprigs of the upper branches!

In the evening we went along with the other pickers to 'The Peacock,' a local public house to drink beer and to reminisce about the day, stumbling back through the apple trees to tumble into our tents and slither into our sleeping bags in the intense darkness of the orchard.

Morning was soon upon us and the urgency of getting underway; completing the first pick was imperative. Forget the misty morning, the cool damp bark and the drenched leaves dripping droplets of diamond crystal and beads of pearl. Tom was always late getting up. He liked his bed and started slowly, preferring to chat to Wilf in the tent beside him, before getting underway.

Wilf dressed in an army uniform of boots, beret, trousers, and jacket, all in army khaki. He was a thin, wiry man with a dark moustache and as Tom said mischievously, 'don't you think he looks like Montgomery?'

'Vaguely Monty,' I ventured. Then I chivvied him up.

'Come on Tom, the day'll be gone; we've got apples to pick. ' I looked at my watch. Tom never wore a watch.

'Just one more ciggy; anyway I'm chatting with Wilf,' he replied nonchalantly.

'I'm on my way,' I responded, snappily. 'I'll see you there.'

Tom was so irritating. Always on about his football, his rugby and his cross country running in Dodworth; always the big guy, drinking, smoking, posing for the girls; but when it came to graft, he didn't 'cut the mustard,' as they say. Yet, there was something charismatic about him; a natural charm and brashness. O.K. he smoked too much, especially in bed, but on the other hand, he did leave his dog ends in curious circles, like Stonehenge! Forget that. Today I needed action, not discussions with Wilf what's-his-name?

In the orchard the gorgeous trees dripped with dew and soon I was wet and cleansed from the smokiness of the fires from the night before. I laboured for about an hour, up and down the ladder, working up a sweat, filling the bag on my back and carefully ladling the green Bramleys into the boxes on the pallets. I enjoyed the physicality of it all; climbing trees was something I always loved and climbing trees to collect treasured fruit was something I truly loved.

In the distance I could see Tom and Wilf dawdling along through the orchard, puffing smoke and laughing together. It annoyed me again to see them together; and Wilf was turning out to be as lazy as Tom. So much for tracksuits and khaki uniforms!

Wilf veered off to speak to some newcomers and Tom met me at the bottom of the tree.

'He's really interesting,' confided Tom in a half tone.

'He's served in Belfast and knew all about the IRA. Amazing stories! He lost a few mates too.'

I ignored his remarks about Wilf. 'Are you going to start Tom, or what?'

'Might do,' he smiled, as he took another cigarette from its packet.

'It's a horr-ible job. I hate it.' He sucked on the cigarette and blew away the smoke.

'But you've only done it for a few days.'

'Think I'll just sit underneath this old tree and wile away the day. I'll tell you what I'm not doing; and that's getting up in those high branches. I'm no Spider-Man.'

'Is it the height of the trees or what?'

'I don't like it that's all. I don't feel safe clinging on to twigs. You can be birdman if you like, but count me out. The bard becomes the bird! Ha!' laughed Tom. '....and to top it all, I think I might be allergic to apples!'

'Allergic to work,' I interpolated sarcastically.

Tom slipped into his humorous 'Dodworthesque' dialect.

'O.K. me oad. Thar's doin' a grand job,' and off he went half way up the ladder.

Minutes became hours, hours became mornings and afternoons melted into days and weeks. It got no better. Indeed apple picking began to be embarrassing with Tom flapping around the base of the trees and myself twitching on the twigs or up and down the wretched ladder.

'Honestly Tom, you are a joke. A big strapping guy like you who can only pick a couple of bags a day. You remember telling me all these stories about hard work and do you know what Tom, matey, you're a fraud, I'm telling you, a bloody fraud, an imposter. Will the real Tom Yarren please stand up?'

'We're on a holiday aren't we? Take it easy. That's what Wilf does.'

'I know what Wilf does. Nothing.'

'He's based at Aldershot, on a placement with the army; just mixing in with the locals. It's part of their training these days. He calls it 'community integration,' they do a lot of it in Belfast.

'Says who?'

'Wilf told me.'

'And you believed him? Listen Tom, he's probably not even in the army.'

'That's typical of you and your cynicism. Always doubting people; always thinking the worst. You feed on it me oad. It's never straight forward with you is it? Honestly, sometimes I wonder why I bothered coming to Kent.'

'I'm not arguing Tom. I'm catching a bus into Tunbridge Wells for a bath and a cleanup. Are you coming?'

Tom didn't respond. 'Alright, I'll see you later.'

It was good to break away, look across the field and empty my mind of foolishness. The bus to the town allowed me to let my thoughts wander across all that Tom had said; about my cynicism and doubts. Perhaps he was right, perhaps he knew me better than I did myself.

I loved the shower, the soap and the sheer joy of feeling clean again. Then the idea hit me! What a fool! Of course! Why not call Aldershot barracks and ask. In minutes I was out of the baths, on the telephone asking the questions and requesting clarification. It had to be done.

On the bus my head was spinning. You win some, you lose some. It can be a funny old world, full of surprises and full of lessons to be learned.

Tom was sitting with Wilf, outside his tent, sharing a simple meal and chattering like two brothers. He looked up as I approached.

'Good bath?'

'Lovely. You should have come with me.'

'Nah. Wilf's been telling me all about Belfast and Enniskillen and his time there. He's going back after this stint.'

Wilf got up and walked across to his tent and ducked his head down to go inside. Now was my chance.

'Tom? I called this guy's barracks; they've never heard of him; there is no such community scheme where soldiers mix in with locals.'

I glanced across to Wilf's tent as he started to emerge, smiling and revelling in now being the focus of our attention.

'I wanted to show you this Tom.'

From behind his back Wilf produced a glistening .303 army rifle fully loaded and ready to go, or that's what he said.

23. <u>Lesson for Life</u>

One of the boyhood challenges for me was to create a weapon that was cheap and reliable. Into this category came the 'staple shooter', a dangerous little catapult which used thin gauge hollow valve rubber attached to a V shaped forked piece of wood which was hand held.

Many of the village boys, myself included, were obsessed with being able to fire a projectile in a reasonably accurate way. I just cannot explain my fascination at this time with this kind of weapon, but I know that at my age it was a compulsion.

We purchased the valve rubber and the fence staples at Abraham Burrell's hardware shop in the village; but it was important never to purchase the two items together because that might rouse the interest of Mr Burrell. The valve rubber should have been used to repair the valves in cycle tyres but a piece of six to eight inches in length would be ideal for the shooter. The staples were in a variety of sizes and always sharp at the points.

When fired, the staple had an unpredictable trajectory, affected by any light breeze and so it was difficult to hit a target successfully over longer distances. We never cared about the staple's wobbling, hissing flight path because that irregular passage was part of the staple's hypnotic beauty and elegance in the air. In the case of a bird in flight, so long as the staple vaguely followed its target, we were satisfied.

Now my step father had already confiscated a really effective catapult which fired the streamlined pebbles garnered from the road called Eccles Row. He took the weapon to his place of work and kept it in his locker. But the staple shooter was hidden in the shed, under a hammer, out of sight, behind the 'winged wheel' moped which he used for work. On the bench was that hammer which had delivered the fatal blow to an adder once menacingly coiled up on our back door mat the previous summer, but that's another story.

One bright morning I went out into the garden and heard the rustling of a bird at the base of the damson and hawthorn hedge between our land and the nursery garden next door. It was a blackbird.

Without further ado I rushed to the shed, shifted the hammer, snatched the staple shooter and grabbed a fistful of staples as ammunition. I was totally fixated with the bird. In my arrogance it offended me.

Into the base of the damson trees, where the blackbird fluttered around, I fired staple after staple at the bird. Never thinking, I became intoxicated with the hiss and ping of the flying staples.

The bird was quickly wounded and once it became a static target, I became sickly and miserable, overcome with the most terrible shame at what I had done. It was appalling. I climbed over the picket fence, invincible against the spiky hawthorn, and found the stricken bird. I held the blackbird in my hands and I filled up with a misery and melancholy. Its sweet head had fallen forwards and lay between my thumb and forefinger.

I shook my head in disbelief and went back to the shed to fetch the spade. I buried the bird at the edge of the garden and only on this day did I confess to my wrongdoing.

24. Guns, Guns, Guns

I never liked guns much; or rather, I perhaps never liked the people that used them. Maybe my dislike came from an experience in the early 1950s while sitting 'minding my own business,' on the wall beside the oily River Medway, when the 'ping' of an airgun pellet struck my upper right arm.

 It hurt like a wasp's sting, but this failed assassination attempt by a secret under cover villager did not bode well for my then future in Wouldham. Who would do such a diabolical thing? How churlish to hide under the cover of the wood and pick off a defenceless target. More importantly, when would the hit man strike again?

For days, nay, weeks I stooped and bobbed, whirled round, hid behind walls, used a branch dragged behind me to obliterate my footsteps and not leave a trail. I changed my routes; changed my voice to a more French sounding tone, not entirely ridiculous, but enough to throw off any would be lurking assassin, who could be skulking and sneaking around the village streets.

At school Mrs Pole, my wonderful teacher, the very woman who had taught me to read and write; she, who believed in me, who many years later in Rochester Post Office, recognised me, and gave me an old shilling, was now having doubts about my character.

Things went from good to satisfactory, the new failure. Even Barry Cornwall who whirled around madly in the playground had noticed the change in me; and the Fleming twin girls and their friend Susie, thought the only remedy was for me to return to the woods and find the very spot the assassin had fired from. Another day, I thought.

A few years later Lee Bussel, the 'fashionista' in 'winkle picker' shoes and a delightful quiff, loaned me a broken Diana .177 air rifle with the mission to complete its repair. Lee and others like him liked guns; Clive Jury for instance, went out at night shooting rats with four tens or twelve bores. But, why Lee thought that I could possibly repair the gun I never knew. I ended up returning the unrepaired weapon and Lee and I went our different ways.

By 1968, my friend Jack Yorkson and I were again travelling across Europe, to rendezvous with a couple of interesting Croatian girls we had met the previous year in Florence. Our earlier meeting on the Ponte Vecchio had been an instant success, even down to the clumsy guitar playing and our puerile banter.

We all seemed to get along so well; especially in the heady warmth of the Florentine evening and the glitter of lights on the shallow Arno beneath the old bridge. This time we, the following year, we travelled in Jack's luxurious Mini, a step up from using the magical hitch hiking thumbs.

The girls lived in Zagreb, in what was Yugoslavia, now modern day Croatia. My pen friend, Srebrenka Saloki, had been in touch through letters and we took up her offer to visit her in a tower block flat at Pazinska 37. In fact Srebrenka's parents and grandparents all lived at the address and this communal living quite impressed Jack and I.

The first morning after our arrival, Srebrenka and Ivana took us to their favourite street cafe to meet their friends, Klara, Petra, Jakov, Tomislav and Marin. Seated outside in the square, we all enjoyed the brilliant sunshine and the conversation, which mercifully was in English.

Srebrenka smiled as she introduced her friends, pausing to mention her boyfriend, Marin. Why would he not be mentioned in any pen letters I thought?

'Marin likes the Mini car,' she said, 'but it's very, how would you say, very typical of England?'

Jack smiled. 'Yes, they're very popular with people, mainly because they're cheap to maintain, not too expensive on petrol.'

'Ah,' retorted Marin provocatively, 'good for you capitalists eh?'

'Good for capitalists,' said Jack, 'good for anybody,' I added.

Tomislav shrugged his shoulders and grimaced. 'It's O.K. for you; and perhaps it boosts the economy, but does it raise the general standard of living for ordinary working people? I don't think so!"

'We are ordinary people, Tomislav,' I countered.

'And you drive round Europe each year?' added Jakov

It was in this withering atmosphere that the blissful rendezvous between Jack and I and Srebrenka's friends, we witnessed the earlier pleasantness of a glorious morning in Zagreb, rapidly begin to evaporate in the face of continued icy comments from Srebrenka's friends.

Jakov waded in, 'well the Mini car company is privately owned I guess, so profits go to the rich; those who own the shares.'

'That's how it works in U.K.,' continued Jack.

'Not here,' said Marin, 'perhaps we should have told you,' he continued, 'we are all members of the Socialist Federal Republic of Yugoslavia aren't we Srebrenka?'

'Yes' interrupted Srebrenka, 'we're all members of the Yugoslav communist party.' Why had she never mentioned that before?

The warm atmosphere immediately became more interesting and less certain, lukewarm; awkward, with irreconcilable chasms beginning to open up; long silent understandings between us began to flounder and sink; the darkness came down over the beautiful memory of a night in Florence.

'We must make a move,' said Jack. 'It's been great talking to you.'

I stumbled on. 'We saw lots of stuff going on in France a while ago. Student protests, violence; they were ripping up all the pavements.'

'It's our year...., but now we drive on to the coast, to Rijeka.

' We swallowed our feelings, thanked our hostesses said our goodbyes to the crowd, climbed into the Mini and were gone.'

We swam in the sea at Rijeka and Jack paddled our inflatable boat towards Krk while I swam towards the island. Only my friend's warning about a large sharp fin projecting from the water fifty yards away, caused me to speedily leave the water.

That night we slept outside amid the rocks, watching Rijeka's clear black night sky, peppered with stars, cut across from time to time by random shooting stars. It was a magical time and an opportunity to reflect on our Zagreb experience. We decided that Vienna would be our next stop, on to our ultimate destination: Prague.

The next morning Jack drove on and gradually the day ebbed away. Darkness fell and it was time to find a place to sleep. We settled on a track way which arched into a secluded forested area. We drove into the trees, into the bowels of the earth, until we could not be seen from the road.

'As it's my car I get to sleep in it,' said Jack.

'O.K.' I responded, 'I get to sleep outside.'

The night was warm and balmy; the sky around us unbelievably dark; the luxuriously warm and comfortable sleeping bag meant the deepest sleep possible awaited me. I dreamed and dreamed while the dark hours passed.

Sometime in the early morning, as the very first light penetrated through the trees in the faintest and weakest of shafts I sensed the strangest of feelings on my face. Like an insect or plant or something more defined and hard upon my cheek, nudging, patting, and poking.   At first my senses failed to respond to the now insistently harsh, prodding metal.

I opened my eyes and standing over me with their sub machine guns, were four soldiers, one poking my cheek with the cold, brutal barrel of his gun. My eyes would surely have revealed the terror and fear I felt throughout my being, for to be staring into the barrels of even one lethal gun was terrifying in the extreme, but so many guns, guns, guns!

Jack was awake and together we offered the soldiers some cigarettes, while they pointed out that we had rested overnight outside the perimeter fence of a Yugoslav military installation and our attention was quickly directed to the rotating radar.

Placated, the soldiers soon continued their patrol, especially after some cigarettes and after we indicated that we were packing up our belongings and moving on. Soon we were gone.

We drove up to Vienna and then onwards towards Prague. As we approached the capital we were stopped at a railway crossing and watched the massively long train slowly pass through with a Russian tank on every bogie, each sporting the red star of the USSR. Mr Alexander Dubcek would get a big surprise! We had a surprise too, because we were turned away immediately for not having a visa for entry. Back to Vienna? No, onwards to Budapest, capital of Hungary!

We came to the border and of course it was manned by Russians. Jack and I were separated, searched, interrogated about our family trees, 'what was your grandmother's name on your mother's side and where did she come from? What was your grandfather's surname?'

We were fingerprinted and our passports taken; and the car emptied to the point where all our belongings, car seats and anything detachable was out on the road. They let us go through in the Mini, but at each bridge and each junction, stood a Russian soldier with his machine gun pointed directly at our faces. Subsequently each soldier followed us in a threatening arc as we continued on our journey.

I recall travelling along a flat, massive valley, meeting lorries stuffed to the gunnels with women in overalls, who clearly were agricultural workers. We paused for food, parked the Mini in the car park and puzzling over the restaurant menu, eventually ordering our food by sticking a pin into our unknown choices. On leaving the restaurant we had to deal with a large admiring crowd around the car and a peculiar round of applause.

Eventually we approached the bridge over the Danube and smiled at the Russian red star on the archway. After entering the city we noted the Hungarian army working on the roads while their Russian counterparts were guarding the important installations. Guns, guns, guns!

Jack stopped the car and went into a news agency. Very soon he emerged with the proprietor who gave us both a box emblazoned with many souvenir coloured photographs, and finally asked us if we were 'Inngleesh.' When we agreed we were, he wildly shook our hands and patted us on our backs. He pointed out that due to censorship, when we sent the postcards on to England we could only use five words as a greeting. When I filled in my card to my parents I remember exactly what I said:

'Five words only. Love John'

25. Kenyan Collage

On arrival in Nairobi in 1973, I was booked into a city hotel, ready to meet with Fred Royce, a director of the Mombasa School and the man who had interviewed me at the Shell Centre in London a fortnight earlier. The school itself had a partnership with Royal Dutch Shell.

While waiting to meet with Mr Royce, I asked at reception if there was anything worth visiting nearby, and the concierge mentioned a meeting in Uhuru (Freedom) Park where the President of Kenya, Mzee Jomo Kenyatta was about to speak. Presumably, he would be speaking in both his tribal tongues of Kikuyu and Swahili, so I probably would not understand a word but to my mind, it was well worth being there!

As I approached the massive crowd, heads began to turn and I slowly started to realise that as far as I could see, I was the only identifiable outsider in the crowd of thousands. I was identifiable by my clothes, my shoes, my walk, but mostly by my fair hair and pale, freckled skin. I did not feel threatened or vulnerable in any way, but made my way through the adoring throng, to get a better view of the President.

Mzee Kenyatta was at the podium, supremely animated and vigorously waving his flywhisk and bakora (walking stick). He was leading the crowd with cries of 'harambee,' (we all pull together) and he seemed to be fueled by the responses of the throng, by the wave of the rungu (club) and bakora.

'Harambee,' he intoned, 'Harambee,' he repeated, and the crowd responded with their chanting; 'Harambee,' they echoed. I turned to the nearest Kenyan. 'What does 'Harambee' mean?

'We all pull together,' he replied, smiling. I joined in. I liked the word 'Harambee' and most of all I liked what it meant. I began to warm to my newly adopted country and in particular, its people.

On Sunday morning, Royce eventually arrived and seemed genuinely pleased or perhaps relieved, to see me, and believe me; I was genuinely pleased to see him! Royce's bearded face looked something like Frans Hals' famous 'Laughing Cavalier,' and his love of amateur dramatics seem confirmed for me, by his demeanour and appearance. He was wearing what I was to discover, was the 'obligatory,' khaki 'safari suit' with a patterned maroon neckerchief at his throat. On this Sunday morning he was keen to show me his new Mazda car, and put it through its paces on the road to Mombasa.

Royce seemed highly strung, intelligent and witty but he was on first impressions a businessman, one whose starting point was to make a good living from his wealthy parent patrons; rather than as an educator. Money, not learning, fuelled him.

He talked about the school, about the elderly Head teacher Mr Peter Paradise, Royce's love of acting, Kenyatta and politics, the bungalow I was to live in, the 'Mombasa Club' and the compelling case for me to become a member. Above all he spoke about himself and his ambitions for the school and the parents who were its wealthy patrons. He also had plans for productions at school and at the 'Little Theatre Club'.

At one point he was so animated about his new production of 'A Man for All Seasons,' and how he would play the part of Sir Thomas More, that, as he leaned towards me, he took his eyes off the road, and almost collided with an monstrous ostrich which attempted to cross at that moment. Bird brain!

For the first few weeks I would live out of my suitcase at a pleasant corner hotel opposite a graveyard; and during the first evening, I strolled across to read the stones and get an idea about the town, by discovering who was buried there. There was a wall parallel with the pavement and beyond were numbers of grapefruit trees in full leaf. To my surprise, there were many English names on the headstones and for my imagination there were many fallen, yellowing grapefruits lying among the graves, like so many skulls.

Teaching at the 'Mombasa School' was challenging at first, but with some helpful advice from Pete Paradise, Mrs VeraTekle and of course, Gary Hawks, I began to slot in. Staff membership of the 'Mombasa Club', situated near Fort Jesus was mandatory and part of the school package.

The food was near perfect, far better than student fare; and it was where I tried all the exotic and expensive foods which, until then, I had only heard about. The waiters took a food and drink order but no cash was ever involved. We members signed a 'chitty' confirming what we had consumed and received an 'account' at the end of each month. But I hated the place. The ex. patriot smell permeated everywhere; the elitism, the classism and racism. Airmail copies of London newspapers, billiard rooms exclusive to men; the snoring and sneering looks of grey haired, ex public school boys, washed up on the shores of the Indian Ocean. It was simply not me.

At school Gary insisted, 'You need a servant,'

'No, I do not. I've survived years as a student without anyone clearing up behind me.'

'It's different here. Who's going to do your washing and ironing?'

'Well, I will.' I replied adamantly.

The truth was that I felt awkward about the whole idea of having a servant. Despite what my mother once said, I had never had or wanted people to 'wait on me', I was very proud of my independence. The word 'servant' had so many negative colonial connotations which I found distasteful and even disgusting. 'Servant,' 'service' 'servile' ugh! O.K , like Ireland, the British had been there before, Kenya had been an ex colony but... I somehow felt tarnished by those who had gone before; and began to feel in some way responsible for the colonialism I detested.

'Look on it this way,' said Gary, 'you are earning a good salary and you can give some Kenyan person some work. Do you realise how important that is?'

'I'll think about it,'

Mary began working at the bungalow the following week and we 'conversed' together, with me following her around, choosing words from my Swahili phrase book. I gathered that she had a very large family, walked six miles to get to my residence and always wore the same green dress and flip flops.

The bungalow was quite traditional, with no ceiling just prepared tree boughs and a makuti (cocoanut leaf) thatched roof, alive with funny geckoes, to which I always loved to give personal names. Below, a mosquito net hung over the bed; the floors were red painted cement and the doors were so badly fitting, with large gaps at the floor were sufficient for a giant Kenyan millipede to pass under. The garden was full of pawpaw, mango, banana, dwarf coconut, giant spiders and red-cheeked cordon bleu birds.

Mary visited once a week to clean the place and to wash my clothes and for the first few weeks everything went well. I liked boiled eggs and I showed her how to prepare them; so it was boiled egg for every visit. Then things went somewhat awry: the bed was left at an odd angle in the room; the mirror was not level on the wall; the wardrobe was pulled out.

I stood alongside Mary and straightened the mirror. 'Like this,' I said emphatically. 'Like this.' Yet when I returned from the school in the afternoons, everything was crooked or jutting or leaning. It was frustrating, so at work I walked across to Gary's maths classroom to find some answers.

'Gary, can you give me a little insight here? Mary has a problem with putting things away as she finds them. I just can't understand her.' I then went on to give him some examples. 'What's wrong with her?' I queried.

Gary paused and smiled. 'When you look at what she does, like that, I agree, it doesn't seem to make too much sense, but think about it; she's showing you that she has cleaned, by leaving items at an angle.....not putting them back as they were. It shows she's done the job.'

I struck myself across the face. 'Idiot!' I yelled out, and puzzled students, in the corridor, inquisitively looked through the glass door panels.

Later on Mary started to steal milk from the fridge, bread from the cupboard and tea from the caddy. I protested to Gary that I was employing a thief.

'She sees the remains of things as hers, by right; you are rich and she is poor,' he said. 'Just leave the remains aside and tell her to take them.' I did as he suggested and set aside all the left overs and remnants. She never took anything again except the remnants. I was a fool; but I was an improving fool.

Christmas 1973 was quiet, as I spent it alone in Mombasa and as a treat for myself, quite early in the day, I decided to walk the few miles to the rowing club and have a celebratory drink and something to eat.

I arrived at the club to be met by the 'door man.' He looked me up and down. 'Sorry sir, you can't come in. You're not wearing a tie.'

I didn't argue with such pointlessness on Christmas Day and somewhat downcast I walked back to the bungalow. By the next morning I had read Anna Karenina cover to cover.

On weekends and holidays, swimming, snorkelling and drinking were de rigour and when Californian, Brian Lincoln arrived at the school it opened up many more possibilities. Brian's alma mater had been in Berkeley and he was there during the troubles, so he came to the school fairly 'fired up'. His father, Professor Lincoln, worked for the I.M.F under the auspices of the U.N. and with Brian's mother, lived in Nairobi. It was thanks to their kindness that Brian and I regularly went away with them on safari (journey) to Tsavo.

Brian had two assets: confidence and persistence and two liabilities, humility and learning. He confidently spoke about Shakespeare but appeared to know very little about his works or anything much connected with the bard; and when I mentioned soccer and tennis, his estimate of his ability hugely outweighed his performance.

I can remember entering Tsavo game reserve for the first time and spotting a cheetah padding parallel alongside the Land Rover.

'Cheetah!' I gasped, 'there,' and I pointed directly at the window. The Lincolns sitting in the front, missed the sighting, but Brian saw it, but he had to refer to his guidebook for confirmation. Put your hand up if you do not know what a cheetah looks like!

I recollect him putting his motorcycle in for a service but suspicious that the work had not been properly completed asked me to inspect.

'Can you check that the mechanics have put in a new spark plug?'

They had not; so Brian headed for a confrontation with the garage and when his money was not refunded, he simply picked up some of their tools and walked away with them as compensation.

At the local restaurant, the coffee was of poor quality and Brian was not content with dressing down the waiter, he insisted on calling up the manager and giving him a noisy, uncomfortable and very public rebuke.

But there were many sides to this man: Brian befriended one of Mombasa's many prostitutes and he really deeply, liked her, perhaps even loved her. She told him all about her village, hundreds of miles away and her journey into the city to earn money to feed her son and support her parents in the countryside. A few weeks later Brian told me that he had paid for his lady friend to enrol on a secretarial course at the local college and a later on, that she had qualified, was in employment and had lost touch.

Brian and I regularly went to Tsavo and he proved a loyal, principled, friend and companion. The two of us heard the coughing of lions at night and saw the scorpions under our groundsheets; we recoiled from the creepy Cretaceous or jaw grinding Jurassic crocodiles which slithered menacingly, thrillingly, towards us at the Tsavo River's edge. I always carried a stick, just in case one of those prehistoric monsters decided to become too friendly; and one of the facts of life dawned on me; that humans are frail, weak and vulnerable and in a straight one-on-one with any of these African beasts we would be annihilated entirely. It was our intellect which separates us from animals.

On another occasion we discovered a small cavern, with dense overhanging vegetation beneath a collapsed bridge structure. With a torch we stepped inside, unaware of what might lurk within the dark and musty cell. The floor was soft, like a carpet of mushy leaves, and as the entrance behind us became smaller, with each step, the folly of our actions began to dawn upon us. What if, a snake, spider, leopard, bushbuck, buffalo or hyena inhabited this space?

Suddenly there was a cacophony of sound, as thousands of flapping wings rippled the dank air. Bats! Bats everywhere! Brian and I turned our backs and looked towards the white sphere of light, now splattered with countless specks, like tea leaves on a white tea towel. Bat wings slapped and whacked our cheeks, our chins, necks and ears. Of course, the soft leafy carpet was guano, bat droppings, and there was much bat mucus deeper in the cave from the carnivorous or fruit eating bats flying outside like a wave from the sea.

Together we watched the superficially infinite, but deeply finite, lines of wildebeest, or zebra and giraffe, antelope or elephant meandering their way to the watering wallowing holes. I told him about a huge bull elephant which managed to creep silently up behind me, and startled, no, shocked me, with its ability to be so clandestine. An elephant on tiptoe?

On another occasion we visited the larger Tsavo east which is mainly flat and has baked dry plains which are cut across by the Galana River which led us to the Yatta Plateau and the unique Lugard Falls.

When one stay was over, the Lincoln's left us at a bus stop beside the road, on the way to Mombasa. I recall leaving my rucksack on the opposite side of the road, ready to hitchhike. Instantly a giant of a baboon seemed to take an interest. I called out.

'Oi! Don't even think about that rucksack; it's none of your hairy business matey!' No response.

'Are you listening?' No response. 'I said, are you listening buddy?'

'He's not listening,' enjoined Brian.

The primate beamed me a withering, dismissive look and then started to undo the buckle and strap which held the bag together. The crafty, 'couldn't care less' male grinned, and showed his awesome array of splinter-sharp teeth. I pointed in his direction.

'Leave it alone! It's nothing to do with you!'

But it was 'to do' with my bumptious baboon, and he was determined not just to open the bag, but to steal the contents and then dive into the nearest tree, where he could leisurely mock my efforts and consume his spoils. I crossed the road to confront him, but not entirely convinced that he would 'back down.'

My fears were unfounded and he did indeed relent; and with breathtaking agility, the baboon climbed into a nearby tree to weigh up his options. I smiled at the sheer joy of the moment. I picked up my bag and put it onto my back. 'Game over!' I said to him. 'Finished?' said Brian.

That night we both went to one of the local beach hotels to watch a young lady who was performing with her pet pythons. They were indeed her pets as they were kept in her house and she confirmed that she felt safer with their protective presence. Brian and I were very supportive and we hoped her dances would be popular with all the mainly foreign visitors to our 'mead hall.'

The girl seemed very different and brave and exotic, but things started to go wrong when a table of eight overseas visitors, noisily started to behave disrespectfully and suggestively; calling out and making rude comments. In their drunkenness they did not see the rising tide of anger in the girl as she elegantly and skilfully moved the python to the rhythm of the music. Brian and I, like two Geats from Beowulf, could see the steam from her kettle.

The crescendo of raucous voices ebbed over the other patrons and occasionally the odd suggestive word was directed at the girl. Like a demented being, she exploded into action, and taking the immense coiled beast from around her neck and arms, she threw her Grendel into the middle of the visitors' table. After all, they were noisy, ignorant and drunken revellers.

What followed was a freeze frame of sheer pandemonium as the visitors fell backwards from their chairs, their beer and bottles violently cascading onto the floor and their bodies wriggling like diminutive eels, squirming to evade the writhing python which quickly followed them to the floor, ensuring sheer terror would enfold them.

Towards the end of my time in Kenya, Brian and I shared a large house, near to the school, as part of a 'house warming' arrangement. In short, I was approached by an elderly Englishman who was a pilot at Killindini harbour; and asked if I would live in the house while he and his wife were on holiday back in England. We would ensure the security of the house, the servants and all free of rent.

A few weeks into our stay found Brian and I relaxing on the upstairs balcony, discussing the state of the world and drinking wine. In a nearby tree I noticed a snake; glossy green in colour and with a lighter greenish-yellow underbelly. It was perhaps four and a half feet in length and was cautiously and gracefully, making its way up and across the branches, the tips of which touched our veranda. I knew that this snake was an arboreal species and that was where it was. I had never before seen a green mamba, but something visceral signalled to me that this snake was exactly that; a green mamba. I pointed.

'Brian, what do you think? Is that a green mamba?' Off went Brian and quickly came back flicking the pages of, 'African Reptiles and Amphibians' until he located the 'Eastern Green Mamba.'

'They are fast snakes, capable of 7 mph.......jeeez, jeeez, it's a Mamba, it's a green Mamba, man... and if cornered they may suddenly become very ferocious and strike... er.... er.. repeatedly in quick succession. The eastern green mamba is an especially venomous snake.'

We evacuated the balcony and watched through the window while the beautiful, deadly beast, the lethal leviathan slithered across the seats where we had been relaxing. Its destination seemed to be the tree on the opposite side of the veranda. We reported the incident to the gardener.

Within a matter of minutes, the gardener and a couple of others, had bullied and hooked the great snake from the tree, and before I walked away, in despair, from the balcony, I saw them battering the reptile to death upon the ground.

Brian and I sat in the living room. He wanted to tell me he had been to look at a flat, and liked it. The owner said he could stay overnight and Brian complained how there had been a partially successful attempt to 'pole fish' him during his time asleep.

I was intrigued to find that pole fishing was obviously the use of a pole, passed through any mesh hole in the window, with the objective of catching a pair of shorts, or shirt or better still a wallet. Some poles had broken pieces of razor sticking out of the wooden stem in case the victim woke up during the theft. Brian rode his motorcycle home but had lost his shorts and shirt and returned home singing, 'California Dreaming,' in his underpants and sandals. He liked that song.

The last time we were together was in Mombasa standing on the corner waiting for the cavalcade to pass. It was a nuisance really, as all the traffic was at a standstill, and nothing moved because of the numbers of Kenyans standing on the pavements. No cavalcade. People were restless, wondering, waiting for the limousines to drive passed. They would at last get a glimpse of him; the man who was always in the news and about whom they had heard so much.

At first came the police outriders, blue lights flashing and sirens wailing and behind them in the first stretched black limousine, sat the President of Uganda, Idi Amin, waving lazily almost laconically at the crowds. Our eyes met.

Kenyans had received scores of refugees fleeing Uganda, from 'beautiful Kampala' and its surrounding countryside. I had spoken personally with many who had lost family members, and recall their horrific stories of those they loved, whose mutilated bodies were found in the river.

I had raced Brown Ndolo's, Mazda against my Super Six Suzuki 250; I had made a great friend in Tad Killani, played some soccer with Hamsa Jeka, out in the countryside on the bumpy pitch and handmade goals and nets. I still recall the goat grazing at the corner flag as we kicked off, and the whoops of the Kenyans as the mzungu pulled on his shorts over his white legs and scored one goal!

Why Fred Royce cast me as the villainous, ruthless, Sir Richard Rich, in 'A Man for All Seasons,' I would never know, for it was Rich whose betrayal would lead to a better man's execution.

26. The Post Office Girl

One of the most intriguing things about life in early seventies Mombasa was that communication by letters or parcels from overseas was not facilitated by a postman. The Post Office did not deliver letters and parcels to houses, apartments, or in my case, the bungalow beside the 'Mombasa Little Theatre.' Instead, there was the simple but practical idea of having a personal post box where Kenyans or blow ins like myself could call and collect at Digo Road.

It was on one of my sorties through the colourful, busy crowds of the town, to the post office, that I saw a lone Kenyan girl lying full stretch on the pavement. She was young, perhaps about thirteen, but she looked to be in her thirties. Her face, once pretty was now battered and lined like a damaged broken stump of a statue; her nose, her ears, her fingers, her thumbs, eaten away by the caustic ravages of leprosy.

Dull, vacant eyes gave away the submission of her spirit to the relentless, ruthless killer that fed on her. Her dusty tangled hair, her toothless, tired grimace revealed no resistance, only hopelessness. The beast was on her, beside her, inside her; consuming her, feasting on her.

The colourful crowd, mainly women, fluttered and flittered like exotic butterflies, in their striped, brightly coloured kikoys and brilliant, dazzlingly patterned kitenges. All were busy, too busy to pay attention to the young, beleaguered girl. Indeed they looped around her with barely a glance. She was an outcast, a pariah, cast aside by humanity, ignored and defined by her illness.

Above her, the blazing African sun roasted us all. The crowds swirled like sandstorms, like hurricanes surging towards the market place, too busy to stop; too busy to help her.

Pundits would call it 'an overwhelming, challenging, human tragedy' but there were many like her; beggars, rough sleepers with little boxes or caps with a few Kenyan coins for their day in the sun.

Only yesterday I had seen a mob of beggars crossing in front of the Castle Royal hotel on Moi Avenue to the baker's shop on the opposite side of the carriageway. It was the end of the day and the baker's hard, dry bread would be manna for the hungry of Mombasa. The beggars crossed the road on all fours, like terrible insects, with cut pieces of car tyres strapped to their knees and elbows. Motorists swerved and hooted, cursed and shook their fists as the front runners and stragglers made it to the shop and the baker's bounty.

In my morning journey to school, I walked passed a young, upright Kenyan man who sat in the shade of a small shopping arcade.. I was moved to give him a coin each morning in payment for the lesson he always taught me. He had lost his limbs through leprosy and sat on the stumps of his rump. He always wore a white shirt and a formal tie. Every morning he greeted me with the broadest of smiles and the most vigorous and cheerful of greetings:

'Jambo Bwana! Habari yaku?'

I learned a lesson I would carry in my heart for ever, namely that I would never complain or feel 'hard done by' and if I did slip into self pity, I would remember my erstwhile friend. How he managed to wear a tie, with his white shirt, and always manage a smile, despite the daily adversity he faced, I could not imagine. It was a priceless lesson. I admire his spirit to this day.

The post office girl lay quietly submissive and defeated. Her head turned sideways, her thoughts seemingly mesmerised by the sandals and flip flops which scuffed their way passed her face. She lay unflinching, almost fossilised.

But she pricked my conscience as I walked into the post office and mouthed my post box number to the teller.

The letter from my parents took me back to Kent; its beautiful hop gardens, the chalky downs, the languorous River Medway weaving its way to the sea. All was well at home.

I sauntered towards the exit and stood outside the doors. Thoughts of Kent evaporated as I reached into my pocket for a coin; anything to assuage my conscience of my own moral bankruptcy. I knew there were cures for this horrific disease. I was educated. I was a school teacher but I was truly ignorant about lepers. I knew of them in bible stories; how people were warned of their coming by a ringing bell but I was unprepared and truly ignorant. They were always pariahs.

My education had in no way prepared me for the girl and her situation. Ignorance and inadequacy strangled me. I felt pathetic and weak. My mouth dried. What could be done to help such suffering and pain? Is life really just a question of money to buy medicines and Aga Khan private hospital care?

I dropped some coins onto her stained blanket. She looked through me in a hopeless way. I turned my head away in distress, for the baby she held, revealed the first tentacles of the disease as he snuggled to her breast.

27. One Evening at the Ferry

It had been a long hot day at the Mombasa School, but despite the rising heat at break time, the students were still cheerfully throwing away the remains of their sandwiches to the monitor lizard which lived under the old school building. The monitor was big and seemed to have adapted very well to its curious environment.

In a former life the school had been a grand colonial house set on stilts on a slight rise of the terrain.

The day always started with the Kenyan National Anthem sung in Swahili which, somehow, I had managed to learn. In the morning session I taught a variety of subjects, all in English, to the youngest students and all based around the English curriculum and modelled on the private school system.

My students were drawn from the diverse communities around Mombasa- French, Italians, Japanese, Israelis, Scottish, Arabs, Kenyans and others. In truth, they were the children of the better off but in common with most children, they had the curiosity to explore and discover the world in which we all lived.

The students' parents were well used to living and doing business in Kenya and their privileged offspring also lived in some comfort. The children experienced an ex-patriot life style and frequented the members-only clubs, hotels and beaches on the Indian Ocean. They knew the ocean by its reefs, fish and crustaceans; they knew the land by its insects, mammals and birds. So what compelled me, a newcomer and ignoramus, to bring in a scorpion from Tsavo in the belief that students would be excited and interested? Naivety is a thin veil to cover the giggles and shoulder shrugging of my unimpressed nine year olds.

Due to the midday heat we finished the morning session at 12 o'clock and all the teachers decamped somewhere for lunch and even a swim. The afternoon session started at 2 o'clock with a group of potential Oxbridge hopefuls who were being fed a learning diet based around the two newspapers 'The Daily Nation' and 'The East African Standard.'

One young orator spoke eloquently about the sanctity of life. Another about poverty, another about how everyone seemed bewitched by material possessions and another who felt that this was not the case in Africa; that there was much more to life than the trinkets of the rich; as typified by the west. It was a lively afternoon with lots of views and opinions expressed and then the students were gone.

The school quickly quietened and an hour passed; the regular inhabitants of the classroom crept out of their lairs and provided me with some lively entertainment. Led by cockroaches; supported by spiders; aided by centipedes and millipedes all like awkward dancers, they accompanied the ticking of the clock with their curiously choreographed ballet inside the belly of the old house.

The caretaker eventually turned me out and smiled as I straddled my Suzuki motorcycle. 'Kwaheri,' he shouted, as I set off for the ferry. 'See you tomorrow Jonathan', I replied.

I approached the Likoni ferry through the avenue of baobab trees and saw a melee of people beneath the control office. An athletic young man was being helped across the road. He was sobbing uncontrollably, shaking his head and wringing his hands.

I spoke to one of the ferry staff and asked what had happened. His response was a curious one and I'll tell you what it was.

There were three Tanzanian friends in the cab of their articulated lorry on their return journey to Dar Es Salaam after delivering their wares to Mombasa.

They had stopped off in the town for a shopping spree and their lorry cab was jam packed with shoes and clothing and other gifts for their families.

The lorry was the first vehicle in the queue and was driven onto the ferry and moved to the front, right up to the security chain. Vehicles continued to be loaded. Without warning the heavy articulated lorry shunted forward with the three friends in the cab. The artic easily flipped off the chain and the lorry lurched forward and toppled off the ferry and into the dark, deep waters of Killindini harbour.

Apparently the lorry floated for some time and then gradually and inexorably sank. The friends went slowly down together and despite the water pressure had managed to open the cab door and all three successfully reached the surface.

In the darkness, one of the three decided to return to the open cab on the harbour bottom, to retrieve a red jersey that he had recently purchased and did not wish to lose. His friend had agreed to swim back down with him.

The tall, athletic young man had gone into convulsive shuddering and shaking; his distress unable to be soothed. The battered remains of his friends were found the following week further round the coast.

28.   The Crater

Ice and snow; no grow on rock and screed. Sickness gurgling deep spirals, deep spiralling; air in misty clouds, hands pale iced.

Choke diesel, smoking fumes, growl of engine. Steeled grubby floor; step up, step up on silver rivets and old tickets strewn underfoot below chugging motor. Bus number, what number? Who cares as you walk on?

Around us misty mountain; giant sleeping; stone head upon stone arms. Inanimate but skin embellished rock and rubble and dried molten chips splintered and smashed.

We slow to ascend. Poles to hold steadily. Touch wrapped aluminium in plastic coat. Beyond window's fingerprints, smudged, smeared, greased blur of life. Can you see the end?

Hunched heads averted. No talk. No touch hand. No smile. Creased padded grimy seats. Chrome hand holds. Waxy with wear. Slowly; millimetre by millimetre. Your perfume. Poster eyes of woman.

No view here. A lake of cloud. Foggy falling cliff. Poor, poor human. What are you? Nausea, wobbling walk. Lie down. Don't lie down. Lie down. Don't lie down. See no plains. No water, no beasts or flying things.

Nothing lives. Glacier moves mimics life. No cells or ooze of life; breath comes hard, choking bus pulling in; go higher, go higher, choices upstairs down, let's go up to finish our love. Lichens on love thousands of years old. Ah glacier, never seen again; just walk, walk from the heights; step off sea level.

Arrive in smoke; walking a young history. Coffee cups jinking in cafes on busy streets, leading to market place; brilliant coloured clothed patterns; black iron bedsteads stacked upon pavements. One upon the other; one upon the other; one-on-one-another. Chinese food a plenty; gaudy market clothes.

We just adventure and other times hiding away is all. We start together and apart ; memories are not enough; and cannot stroke the skin or soothe. Humid, sticky hands not for holding or comfort; dry world like beach. Gradual gradient; do not touch.

Climb lower slopes, rain forest. Our tears. Heath land of savannah; giant heather; and moorland. Rise early. Smiles. Wild alpine flowers; giant lobelia and groundsel. Hoping for summit views; the peak; Kibo.

Crater empty; devastated ; pain; struck meteorite; failedoomed . Low forest, middle heather- moorland; top desert. Colobus, blue monkeys, hornbill, turaco, eagles n buzzards soar high above few tuftsa grass, mosses, lichen, flowers helichrysums and senecios. John Daudi. Guide. Crown of alpine flowers n bus ticket swirls on windy street. Diesel fumes her eyes n few tuftsa grass her hair. Itzover.

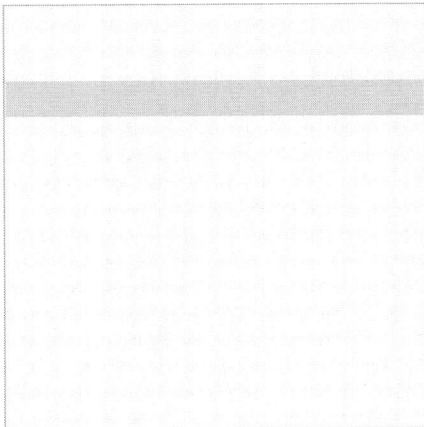

<u>Look outlook out afox.</u>

Look outlook out afox,

Among the orchard trees.

Headrazed, a lert inits haunt;

A bay bee, me, does watch.

Ap pulls gone, an bow low;

Leaf ngrass lush us then.

Arm other whiss purrs, sssh!

No stir, my baby sun.

Afox eyesore, baffled site;

Babe looksout of blew sea eyes.

Two see, an wonder why;

A chance n counter comes.

Bats

Velvet membrane clawed jewelled eye

In trees dangling down eyes all around

Paper bag burger

29. The First Visit

After my return from Kenya in the mid 1970s I squandered some of my assets on a new car. It was a 'white and nice' little Datsun Cherry and just the sort of transport to carry my grandmother and I to Ireland on what was to be the first of my many visits to the beautiful land.

It all started with a weird coincidence when I spoke about how I was to get to Gillingham, to collect my new vehicle and get home. Someone suggested the bus, so I travelled up with Gerald and midway through the journey I was tapped on the shoulder. I turned to see an African guy who asked me if I had lived in Kenya.

'Yes' I replied. 'I was a teacher there.'

'Well I was a steward at the Mombasa Club', he said, and indeed I recognised him. We shook hands. How weird is that?

My Nan and I had soon mapped out our journey up to Wales, where we planned to stay overnight in a hotel before travelling through Anglesey to Holyhead; and finally across on the ferry to Dun Laoghaire. She was determined to take me to our family village in County Meath and also to locations in County Mayo where she lived with my grandfather, after her return from America. I would carry my years of absence, the Irish rebel songs and a vow to only read Irish literature after the age of twenty five with me to the land that I longed to visit.

We were settled into our shared Welsh hotel room and shortly the two of us went downstairs to the bar. It was to be my greatest pleasure to buy a drink for my wonderful grandmother, Mollie Doyle. To see the trials and tribulations of her hard life etched on her face always distressed me – until she smiled. She epitomised the qualities I so admired: industriousness, a sense of adventure, kindness and stylishness.

'I'll have a gin and tonic,' she purred, as she snuggled into the seat in the quiet bar. She was so delighted that she glowed with pleasure.

Three local men were seated at the bar, chattering away, but curiously as I approached, they changed from speaking English to speaking Welsh. From their 'body language,' it was quite obvious that they were including my Grandmother and I in their conversation and that irritated me intensely, to the point where I felt like speaking 'at them' in Swahili. I regretted that the only Gaelic I could speak was, 'dun an doras' (shut the door) which I had learned from my mother and I was certain that it would just would not work on this occasion.

When I returned to my Grandmother and explained my suspicions; she was outraged and I had to restrain her from 'speaking to them.' She was a fighter, indeed! Shortly afterwards she said she would go up to the room to sleep after the long journey. I fled the building to sample the delights of Wales.

The next morning we left the hotel very early and were soon across the Irish Sea and in the port, disembarking. Nan slipped into what seemed to be a familiar route, taking me through Dublin, along the wandering River Liffey, into the Phoenix Park where I gawped at the trees and the green lawns; next, we breezed through to Blanchardstown, on to Mulhuddart, then Clonee, Dunboyne and

Summerhill. Leaving that pretty village we arrived at the junction with Shaw's pub and eventually found the road into Rathmolyon.

Shortly afterwards, we approached the village, drifting round the final corner and onto the main street. Ahead of us were the crossroads. It was exactly as I had imagined it. You know the feeling? When you reach a place you know, before you actually arrive? It was a place intermingled with childhood stories, shrouded and cloaked with characters of myth and legend; names associated with life and fun and vigour and tragedy. People and families were etched or doodled into my memory; they were living or lived in this place; I knew their stories; their narratives were mind-etched; laid down memories like the strata of sedimentary rocks.

The grand house stood at one end. (Was it really threatened by the Black and Tans?) Harper's thatched bar where 'old Jimmy' Harper and Lil Harper lived, in the middle, and at the end there was late Great Uncle Pat's candy shop and his younger brother, Great Uncle Mattie's stone cottage tucked into the edge. The two Uncles had been happily unmarried. Rathmolyon Post Office lay opposite with Mrs. Donachy the postmistress, in charge. My heart leapt. I had arrived!

'You're pleased with yourself,' my grandmother whispered. 'Shall we stop at Harper's? We dallied for a moment to speak to old Jimmy and have some refreshment.

For my grandmother, meeting Mrs. Sweeny and her daughter, Ann Sweeny was a reunion of old friends. They all knew each other especially as my Great Granny, Mrs. Catherine 'Catty' Forde had worked for the Sweenys ever since her husband died from tuberculosis in 1919 and she had been left to rear their three children.

My mother and her sister, my aunt Maeve, had been friends with Ann from childhood. My Grandmother looked forward to a reunion with her younger brother Mattie and perhaps visiting the graveside of her late brother, Pat and also to her mother's resting place.

Mrs. Sweeny was a small, quietly spoken, elderly lady. She spoke very kindly about the world and had a gentle and elegant manner. Ann, her daughter was lively and energetic; full of smiles and questions about the journey, about England, the new car and our arrival.

I introduced myself to Mrs. Alice McGuire and the little crowd of young McGuires who sat in the kitchen, expectantly awaiting some words from this odd English voiced youth. Within the hour I was entertaining them all with an acoustic rendition of McTell's 'Streets of London,' 'like a long haired rock star' or so I was told many years later.

In the kitchen, young Alice McGuire danced and sang that day, and her brother sang a sad lament. I had never been in such a strange, large kitchen with its high ceiling and with a dozen hooks for hanging or curing meat. In the middle of the kitchen stood an old table with six chairs; a cream coloured 'AGA' stood to one side and the pantry stood on the other. An old carver chair, with lots of cushions and shiny with use, was set aside for Mattie McLoughlin, my great uncle.

Looking back now, in time, I realised that it was through a series of tableaux vivant that I best remember Uncle Mattie; and the process of gradually getting to understand my Nan's gentle, younger brother was a difficult mission in the short span of a holiday.

He was at first sight, a slightly built, quiet and unassuming man with the most beautiful turquoise blue eyes. He was of good humour and in his gentle way he made an occasional, well chosen remark which was instantly wise and even profound.

'If a man will steal a pin, he would steal anything,' he said of a local man. I cleared my mind to listen to what he said. So rare was the occasion that all went silent when Uncle Mattie was drawn out to comment.

Mattie spent one night attending to the birth of a calf in the dimly lit, thatched stone barn. I remember looking into the gloomy space in the late evening. There lay a cow on its side, in the straw, enduring the first pangs of birth. Mattie was beside it with his arm around its head like a fresco of the caring shepherd; and the next morning his self deprecating smile spoke volumes about the new arrival, a fine calf.

He wanted to show me Kate Forde's thatched stone cottage with its thick, rough silver-grey walls, deep windows and reedy roof. It lay along the road between Rathmolyon and Summerhill.

'Kate lived there until she passed,' Mattie, mused, 'and then it was rented out and now.....well, there you are....we'll see.'

When we returned to the village he was keen to share a glass of whiskey with me and to colour in some of the story I so longed to hear. It was truly a special time. His cottage was sparse and tiny with a front room and kitchen; there was a through door into what was once the sweet shop; and two tiny bedrooms accessed by a steep, narrow, wooden staircase. It had been purchased in the fifties from a certain Captain Fowler. A few family pieces were dotted about, but typically Mattie was unable or reluctant to speak about anything in the family and I had not yet framed any sensible questions to ask him.

'Shall we go over to the far side?' Mattie asked softly.

'The far side?' said I, in a puzzled tone. 'Oh...across the road.... of course, why not?'

Soon we were over the road into the small, crowded bar, filled with villagers, most of whom, were Mattie's friends and well-wishers. We edged towards the counter and he introduced me as 'the great nephew,' using the word 'great' to denote our relationship and not my status! Villagers circled and whirled around, pushing passed us and forming knots and clusters.

Many looked keenly into my face; some compared Mattie and I out loud agreeing that we looked vaguely alike but one stepped up and said, 'sure he looks like his Great Uncle Pat, God rest him!'

After a while I was approached by Mr. McGrainne, the local grave digger. McGrainne was a grey faced, watery eyed man, who seemed to single me out for his attention- perhaps subconsciously measuring me up for some future assignment- but certainly homing in on me for his own personal reasons.

'Ah, so you're Mattie McLoughlin's great nephew? How old would you be now?' I looked across to Mattie for some help, but he was busily chatting among the melee of villagers.

'I'm twenty five.'

'Ah twenty five; and what do you do for a living?' enquired McGrainne.

'Well I'm a teacher now, but I was at University.....studying and I've been working abroad, teaching,' I replied, rather suspiciously.

'Studying and teaching?' he countered. 'Studying what?'

'History and political philosophy.....education.' I blurted out.

'Ah now then, answer me this: Would you know how to mark out and prepare a grave? To measure and dig it out?'

'No, I wouldn't know what to do or what to excavate I'm afraid; I trained to become a teacher.' I countered, cautiously.

McGrainne paused for a moment; he drew a breath and took a swig of beer from his glass; he sucked the stout noisily through his teeth and swallowed.

'Ah,' he sighed, shaking his head, 'you don't know how to dig a grave?' He shrugged his shoulders. 'So you think you're edu..cate...d?'

He shook his grey head again and with that coup de grace, he drifted away like a ghost, to speak with another villager friend. I pondered my hopeless, deflated situation!

Later that afternoon, I recall Mattie seated up on the tractor, circling like a drifting bird on a thermal, having topped half the field. I watched him for some time and eventually he waved at me by way of acknowledgement. The sun had smiled upon these fertile fields of Meath. It was truly a beautiful place. Why did we ever leave?

'Come over,' he called out, waving one hand over his head. 'Our McLoughlin family motto is: 'we keep our promises.' He stopped the tractor and left the motor ticking over while he spoke.

'Would you mind taking over for a while? I'm going in to get a cup of tea and a sandwich? Promise?'

'But I've never.....' 'Sure you'll be fine....I shan't be long at all.'

He left me there for a good hour, circling with the tractor in ever diminishing circles, hoping the beast would run out of petrol and come to a final shuddering halt, but no such luck. Mattie returned when he returned, and not a moment sooner. I'd kept my promise.

The next day I witnessed another cameo, where Mattie was digging potatoes beside the hedge; carefully stacking them and rubbing away the crumbly soil, from each 'pratie', with his thumb. The image of my Uncle Mattie that morning, always reminded me of the poem, 'Digging,' by Seamus Heaney; and 'by God the old man could handle a spade....' but I never told my Great Uncle that.

Over the next few days we all travelled along the Newline Road to visit the Hill of Tara where the Irish kings were crowned. At Cherry Valley House my grandmother and I were again visited by McGuires,

Fordes and Sullivans. All seemed eager to meet my grandmother and to listen to the strange young upstart from over the water 'who looked like a rock star with the long hair and guitar.'

Everyone seemed keen to tell me about my family to 'weave me into the village tapestry'; to tell me we were renowned as the Rathmolyon blacksmiths, responsible for much of the ironwork in the village and for the shoeing of countless horses.

Apparently we were respected members of the village and seen as honest, law-abiding and god fearing. Indeed one literate family member even wrote up legal documents for those who needed them. Nonetheless, the unique or odd ones in our family were particularly singled out. Take 'The Poultice' for example, with his nickname attributed to his sporting prowess and in his singular ability in hurling to stick so closely to his opponent that he appeared attached like a poultice to a wound.

Another of the family, (for whom I now seemed to have become the responsible spokesperson), was called 'The Dodd' and was such a strange character that: 'he could walk passed you on the street and would not even tell you that your house was on fire!' I would be told many more stories over the years by Mr Desmond O'Rourke and on many occasions was perhaps expected to have an explanation for these behaviours and oddities. What a strange and beautiful crowd I came from! Now reminiscing, I realised I had also fallen into a treasure of a community.

Before too long my Grandmother and I were waving goodbye to Ann and Mrs Sweeny and to Meath. We were on the road to County Mayo, or more accurately, Scrigg, Aughamore, near Ballyhaunis. It would become a journey into the past, to the place where grandmother had settled with grandfather, where my mother and aunt had grown up.

Grandfather Anthony O'Boyle had been the youngest of six boys born to Bartly (Bartholomew) O' Boyle and his Gaelic speaking wife. Presumably because of the very limited chance of being helped by inheritance, he chose to emigrate from Ireland to America to find his fortune. Nothing new in that scenario!

Grandfather travelled around 1912 on the SS Olympic, sister ship to Titanic. In fact his name turned up on the Ellis Island 'Immigrant's Wall.' Apparently, he worked on the roads and buildings of New York; and sometime around 1929 he met and married grandmother at 'Our Lady of All Angels,' in the Bronx.

According to her best school friend, Molly O' Hannon, my Grandmother, although born in Fordstown, County Meath had been obsessed with America, indeed with anything American. Why she was obsessed none could ever fathom, but anyway there was a story from Molly O' Hannon, that, so overwhelming was her obsession, Grandmother had created a stick motif of the letters 'U.S.A.' on the gate leading to her house 'on the boreen' along the road between Rathmolyon and Trim

Fortunately for my Grandmother, Mary Rose McLoughlin, she was in touch with an aunt, Ellen Cosgrave, who lived in a Webb Avenue tenement in the Bronx, and on whom she could depend. Anyway, off she went to America on the Queen Mary, I think.

Rumour has it that she courted a charming New York policeman with Irish roots; that she went to 'speak-easies' and she coped with prohibition, but she never married her policeman but instead chose to marry Grandfather.

My grandmother told me some of this while sitting next to me in the white Datsun Cherry, on the way up to Ballyhaunis; but I couldn't verify any of the information. I would never get to meet or speak to my grandfather and those closest to him were never available to speak about him.

Grandmother painted a horribly mixed picture of the man she had married: one part of him as a charming Doctor Jekyll, the 'life and soul' of any party; dancing on the tables in sheer effusive joy. The other picture was of Grandfather's alter ego, of a Mr Hyde character, who once challenged and assaulted a neighbour for staring over his garden wall at his cattle. Grandmother never mentioned love or romance.

A story circulated about the death of a man on the subway and grandfather's involvement in his death. Grandfather came down to me as a simple but brutal man. Mother spoke of him killing and butchering cattle outside his farmhouse back door, and in front of his two young daughters. Had England made us all soft?

Grandmother painted a bleak picture, but had seemed happy up to the birth of my own mother in the Bronx in 1931. In the middle of '32, Grandmother and mother returned to Mayo for good and grandfather followed shortly afterwards and set about 'building his own house with his own hands.' Soon a second daughter, Mary, had arrived into the troubled household. It was at this early stage in their marriage that Grandmother learned that her new husband had been married before to a local Mayo girl, Amy O'Callan. They had a child, Dervla..........both he had forgotten to mention.

Grandmother and I soon found and visited the huge, derelict house where she had lived when she returned from America. Inside in its spacious, empty, downstairs rooms, the cattle roamed; and muck, straw and mud, was smeared in equal measure. I stood in front of that once grand place; thinking of what might have been; sadly reflecting on the tumble down facade. I noticed a rusty window attachment on the ground and put it in my pocket. I have it now and it always makes maudlin mischief in my mind....

Quickly we left the site and Grandmother showed me the old school, the pathways, the church and the graveyard where we looked for grandfather's grave. She told me about the time when he was so violent that she was forced to take her two daughters and spend the rainy terrifying night hiding in a ditch. My Grandmother had fled the marriage many years earlier, beaten down by Grandfather's abusive behaviour and finding no answer in the law or in the church. For Grandmother the only answer was to run for her life.

In 1947 she came to England with her eldest daughter, my mother, to start her new life. Sadly the youngest daughter, my Aunty Mary was left behind to endure the wrath of my Grandfather. Mary fled to a local nunnery and I still have the letter as proof of her first visit.

30.   The Harvest

One Sunday morning I jumped high enough to head the football onwards to the wide man, but a gentle, unintended nudge, from my airborne opponent, meant that I fell awkwardly on my back and ultimately the game was lost.

Years later a bus load of my school students travelled to visit the newly erected London 'Dome'. On the return journey, a call came in to school reception from the coach driver, about being involved in an argument with some of the male students. The students had been standing up in the back of the coach and restricting his vision. Apparently the driver had stopped the coach and politely, by his account, had asked them to be seated and not to stand and obscure his rear view. They became abusive and threatening; he tried reasoning with them and now he feared for his safety.

The Principal asked me to meet the coach in the school drive and ensure that the bus was safely emptied, the students dispersed and the driver placated. Shortly the coach arrived and passed through the school gates and onto the car park area. I immediately approached the front exit door which the driver quickly opened.

'Thanks,' said the driver.

'You've had a few problems,' I responded, climbing the three steps onto the coach. The driver looked terrified.

'They've threatened me and I'm going to report them.'

'Let me speak to them.'

I looked up along the coach at the same old suspects albeit, with a few new recruits, and, some female support. The atmosphere was bristling and electric. The boys started to move towards the front and the driver; the girls started baying for blood. I stood in the aisle.

'Now whatever's been said here, I'm not happy about.'

I stood my ground as six or seven boys slowly came towards me.

'We will open the rear, emergency door of the coach and disperse through there. I'm sorry but you are not listening. The rear emergency door is open and you can go through that.'

I had no intention of allowing the boys to pass within striking range of the driver, for they were determined to set about him and do him physical harm. This was something I wanted to avoid at all costs. The crowd continued to edge towards me and the leaders were snarling and seeking retribution for what the driver was purported to have said.

'Wait there lads. You know me well. I promise I will speak with the driver and investigate what has happened.'

'He's been disrespectful, sir, disrespectful, and we're going to 'ave 'im, smack him up..'

'We're not going to do that boys. Leave it to me and I'll sort it out.'

To my relief the nearest boys started to pull back and move towards the rear of the coach.

'Go back ,' said the front lad, as he turned. 'Sir's going to sort him out. '

I spoke briefly with the driver about the altercation and listened carefully to his version of the incident. I took his name and number and explained that I would be in touch with his office.

I could see the students like a restless stream cascading from the coach's emergency exit, spilling out upon the car park and up the nearby steps of the walkway, across and over the dual carriageway.

The coach slowly started to move, easing its way towards the gates. I raised my hand to wave to the driver and as I lowered it, I noticed a huge slab of concrete come hurtling through the air, crashing onto the roof of the coach, rolling over the top and falling to the ground. I spun round to glance at the bridge, for it was from there that the projectile had come. I turned again to watch the coach leave, angry that a student had done such a thing.

It was at that moment that a second slab of concrete was airborne and it was this second huge boulder that struck me squarely and spitefully at the base of my spine. My back was on the front line again. Although the pain was excruciating, I managed to convince the school nurse that I could drive home but it was 'provided I presented myself at A&E in Medway.' Her worry was the possibility of a ruptured spleen, but it proved not to be the case.

In the mid 1990s, just to prove a point, I climbed a tree in my back garden, with the intention of pruning. Halfway through the process, and for some inexplicable reason I slipped and fell, landing on my back and striking a large wooden bench.

A lifetime of football and cricket games eventually came to a close in my mid fifties; to be replaced with orienteering, running and eventually cycling. Lots of recreational running, the Maidstone marathon and a few five and ten kilometres marked out that time.

In 2008 there was an opportunity to slip the knot of a stressful job and take on a new challenge by cycling solo 'end to end', Lands End to John O' Groats. It was one of the most marvellous of adventures and worthy of further chatter. The following year, the irresistible lure of the road then took three of us, this time from Mallin Head to Mizen Head 'end to end' in Ireland. In between there was a hike up Ben Nevis.

In 2011 I met up with my first cousin Connor who was visiting U.K. and who I had 'found' but who I not seen for forty two years. We walked together through the woods of Cuxton 2011- visit

Neuro Fiona norwood – eat fat

King's

Changes 2012 cramps hands weight;sleep; hallucinations; hand gestures

Focus on ability, not disability

Dont want my life to be defined by the disease

61 years me / 3 years someone else

Goethe- 'The things that matter most should never be at the mercy of things which matter least.'

Physical 'i've put on weight   'yes but all in the wrong places'

Attitude resilience, resourcefulness, creativity' ecstasy positivity

2013 walking

2014

The future

'save your strength and energy for the things you love doing'

'the barrel of energy

The link physical/cerebral cognitive

The best out of people

students

the second life, at a different level

coming to terms with imprisonment

In mortal combat with the beast;

An enemy that does not sleep.

Ah my sweet love we made a tryst;

That faith and trust we surely keep.

The riddled apples on the bough;

Are nature's bounty nonetheless.

Ah gentle love of sweetest lips;

Our special love is surely blessed.

Like fish in shallows all exposed;

To predators which soar above.

Ah sweetest girl we made a tryst;

That faith and trust we surely love.

The bruised damsons in a sprig;

Each, nature's offspring, infant, child.

Ah precious heart and emerald eye;

Our bubbling joy and brimming smiles.

As sparrows gorge on stubble's stalks;

Blind to brutal hovering hawks.

Ah gentlest girl we made a vow;

That lives and love will beauty show.

The buxom pear it dangles down;

Is nature's queen with curvaceous crown.

Ah lovely wife so sweet and true;

My life was spent just loving you.

The brute it jousts with vicious spite;

The unhorsed warrior put to flight.

Ah stay beside me love so kind;

That peace and comfort we will find.

31. Widows and Wine

In the education arena in the late nineteen nineties there was a secure belief that all students should participate in 'work experience' and this phenomena would gently introduce them to 'the world of work.' I think we all seemed to agree with the notion that 'man is born to work,' so we'd better get started then!

As a principal organiser of work experience, I should have been more prepared for what happened to me in the corridor that Thursday morning, when I was approached by a student called Maria Morse. She was keen to discover if I would be coming along to observe her at her work placement.

As I had been completely focused on co-ordinating the year group's work experience for my colleagues, I foolishly brushed away Maria's question like I was swatting a tiresome fly.

'Absolutely, I always come to speak with students at their placements.... I look forward to it.... and I'll see you there.'

Maria smiled angelically. 'What day do you think you'll visit sir?'

'Not sure yet Maria.....but I'll 'phone them and see when is the best time....don't worry. Are you enjoying the work?'

'I'm really enjoying it, sir. It's what I want to do....but you might not like it sir.'

'No, no, I'm sure it'll be fine....great....look... I'm sorry I have to rush...but I'll see you there. Good luck! I hope it all goes well for you.'

Maria nodded and smiled sympathetically.

I know, for a teacher, the corridor is no place to do business, but often the passing remark, comment, instruction encapsulated in a fleeting moment is all the morsel we might get for that day or week. We've all made important decisions as we pass from one room to another via a corridor and sometimes it's that fleeting remark that stays with us. Maria couldn't possibly know what my likes and dislikes were.

That week was a busy one, and to be brutally truthful, I had forgotten to contact Maria's placement- which was rather like inviting things to go wrong. I did not heed the lessons learned in previous years. Take Gary for example. He decided to contact his relatives in Australia on the company telephone and his placement manager was not amused; and feisty Fiona who had a raging argument with her water company supervisor and was asked to leave the premises.

My personal favourite was Duncan's placement at the local garage. He managed to aggravate the mechanics so much, that they took hold of his legs, turned him upside down and dunked him a couple of times in a barrel of dirty oil. He came out looking like a toffee apple and such a punishment was henceforth referred to as 'dunking Duncan.'

Always in a hurry, I had arranged for the school secretary to check on Maria's and another student's placement, contact them and arrange my visits. The secretary, efficient as ever, organised my visits for Wednesday of the second week, one in the morning and the other in the afternoon.

Wednesday morning arrived and I checked my diary. My first student visit was to a student at a wine storage warehouse, and the second was to the Oakland and Grimm Funeral Directors to see Maria. That could be interesting!

Oh the delicious scents of wine and wood! When contrasted with our school canteen and corridors and classrooms, there was no comparison. The overwhelmingly aromatic wines transported me to France, to an old farmhouse in my dreams.

James, my first student, was the ideal work experience candidate, immersing himself completely in the experience and taking me round his new domain with the confidence of the chief executive. He took me to the rose wines, the whites, the reds, and fizzies. He smiled and seemed proud of his placement, treating the wines as if they were newly won school friends and seeing his task as showing them off to another trusted, older friend. It was a successful experience for James.

An hour later, I turned the car respectfully into Oakland and Grimm, Funeral Directors and I must say felt distinctly uneasy. In the reception area stood a shiny black hearse; and behind the hearse a tall, dark haired gentleman wearing a smart black tailcoat.

I smiled across at him, as he inspected the car.

'Hi there! I'm Mr Malcolmson from Bexling School; I'm here to meet up with Maria. She's on work experience.'

'Good to meet you, sir. I'm Mr Grimm, one of the owners.' He paused for a moment while he considered his next words.

' Yes, Maria.'

'How is she doing?'

'A natural, sir. She's cut out for the work. An absolute natural. Born for the job. Come this way.'

In the doorway of one of the lower floor rooms, stood a smiling Maria, clearly eager for me to see her work, and as her teacher, quite honestly, I was feeling intensely queasy.

I looked out through the window as a spattering of rain splashed across the panes. Weather! I'd heard the forecast. There was lots of rain in Colerain, snow on Snowdon, hale in Halesowen, wind on Windermere, sleet in Sleet Cove and ice in Eisteddfod. English weather.

Maria directed me through the door. My hands were clammy. My head dizzy. There were two snow white, dead bodies, lying on beds, both with towels covering their midriffs. I looked at the lifeless faces and like a conveyor belt my mind ran images of lives lived. The air felt heavy and choking.

'I want to show you my stitching, sir,' beamed Maria as she pointed towards the first corpse, indicating the neat line of stitches like the lacing on an old fashioned corset.

'It's very tidy Maria, very tidy.' I swallowed hard, and realised I didn't know how to appraise such an effort.

'....and this one over here, sir. This one took much longer.....'

I looked across at the anonymous face; someone's father or brother or son. I looked at the regular pattern of the stitches and the care that Maria had taken on each one.

'Wonderful work Maria.'

'Thank you, sir, for coming.'

'I wouldn't have missed it Maria,' I lied.

32. Not the Bald Guy?

I grew up knowing little about my father. He had been an indistinct shadow in my life. True, I spent time on his blue and white boat while he wore his captain's cap and called out to his three Alsatians to plunge into the muddy River Medway. True, he always chivvied them all to join him and only Judy, his favourite, plunged in and swam pluckily towards his boat.

True, there was always the nagging question about what had happened after my parent's divorce. My mother for all her strengths would never share a word or photograph or letter or anything at all about him. She had quietly destroyed them all. Perhaps she had even destroyed the memories themselves.

It was also the case that I often felt like an outsider either because of the split between my two biological parents or the addition of a new step father in my life or the enduring effect of an unsettled childhood; the different heritage learned from my mother and grandmother and aunt. It was always there in the background. Maybe we got this way because of that.

They say the Irish have long memories. My mother's and grandmother's went back a long time, in a shared and difficult history. Most of this tricky period centred on a crowded time between the age of three and six. It was the transition time when the arguments were bad and the world within the walls of the old cottage was sour.

Father took me from school one day, and it gave me the chance to be an adventurer, but also to make an important decision. At the mighty age of five he took me to his parents' home in Fulham.

The terraced house smelled stale as both my grandparents smoked heavily and relied on Foxes glacier mints to keep their young grandson quiet and happy. I slept with father on the black and white striped, dingy mattress, on the front room floor; but I never really knew him. I never really knew them either. On the train back to Aylesford, he asked me who I would like to be with.

'John would you like to live with your Mother or with your Father?'

I didn't realise that this answer would predetermine my life from that time onwards. A plume of silver steam drifted by our carriage window and I paused in thought for the moment. I chose my mother. He dropped me off at our tumble down cottage and I never saw him again.

Having a new step father, however nice it sounds, was never like a new car or new house and it never suited me. Somehow I never got the hang of taking on the role of stepson. I tried my best of course but my sister Kiera was different. She managed the whole enterprise so easily and so sweetly. She was that bit younger and that bit better at it.

Changing my name from Dobbs to Devreaux was shockingly traumatic and painful. What's in a name? What was the meaning of the word? Were we really the 'Dobbs' as folklore had it: the small grotesque supernatural creatures that make trouble for human beings? A rose is but.....

Whatever happened to Dobbs? All my certificates and school reports were in the name of Dobbs and all would eventually be changed on the instigation of my mother. The scissors would cut the cord. Hours would be invested in the surgery; cutting out the name Dobbs and sticking on a patch of paper with the Devreaux name. Then it's done; or is it?

The bad news was that adoption by my stepfather was not an option. The costs were high and motivation low. So my new name would be simply assumed. I would become 'known as' Devreaux. It had been a well known even unforgettable appendage. George Devreaux was apparently a famous musician in music hall....

In all the fuss my middle names couldn't be hidden: George and Malcolm; George, after my Granddad; Malcolm, after my father. What a legacy!

The name changed on the school register but the rubbish kept coming from those who thought that torturing someone with a new name, an odd name and a forsaken name would be fun. It wasn't.

Well life went on, and two more sisters were born; there were not even random comments from my mother, or my grandmother, to provide any insights for me. Secrets were secrets; locked was locked; shut was shut. The identity of Malcolm Dobbs, my father, was destroyed; the unperson, created. Like the inevitable tightening of a terrible tourniquet the 'unthink' began to strangle me, cutting off the oxygen of reason. Enter newspeak.

The unperson with his few miserable years would never leave my mind. On the endless cross country run; the interminable rain drenched soccer game; the brutal fight in the recreation ground; the unperson would never flee my memory, but entered like a ghost; his face shattered and unrecognisable like the spewed up tesserae of a broken mosaic.

In the end the sheer unfairness of it all was truly motivational; for it is in adversity that we discover our true natures. Unlike many around me, it was the cruel brutality of the wilderness, which had triggered an authentic strength.

Gradually, time erased father's features; his face, his voice, his walk, his gestures, his laugh, his glance, and his memory. He walked away from us and never attempted to communicate or contact me again. More years sidled by; and his face had gone: erased, rubbed out; brushed and blasted away; scrubbed, seared, scorched, scraped, censored, expunged, obliterated, annihilated. But the unfinished business remained.

Over the many ensuing decades I secretly searched for signs of my father in many visits to the Public Records Office, letters to possible sources like the Salvation Army or Military Records. I kept it all secret because of my parents and their lack of understanding or sympathy with my search. I even hired a private investigator who took my money and led me to a bogus address near Birmingham.

The mystery deepened as I found that both my grandparents had passed away; and still I could not find records of my father anywhere. 'Dobbs' was a fairly common name; not like Smith or Jones or Williams or at least, common enough. Most of all I wanted some information or even a precious photograph of my father, any of which would help to create 'closure' as they call it nowadays.

I once found an old photograph showing my Aunty Maeve and Uncle Ferdinand after getting married. There appeared to be a young man on my mother's arm as the celebrating party walked through Maidstone.

When my mother visited my house, I pointed to the young man in the picture and asked her:

'Is that my father?'

'What do you think?' answered my mother.

'Well, I'm asking you the question, Mum. Is that my father?'

'What do you think?'

'You were there Mum. Is that Dad on your arm?'

No prizes for her response.

One fine day found me again looking for the existence of my father at the Records Office, searching the marriages section, for it was likely that my father had remarried but naturally I did not know to whom. Then at a magical moment there appeared a corresponding entry on a marriage certificate. It was 'Garner Dobbs.' I requested a marriage certificate; he had married 'Gay', so I looked for children under 'Garner Dobbs' and 'jackpot!'

The addition of 'Garner' had been a 'game changer,' because it placed 'Dobbs' under the 'G' of Garner, rather than the 'D' of Dobbs in any index. Garner had been the maiden name of my father's mother. Intriguing! It seemed to cover my father's tracks, but why?

I immediately discovered the birth of a half-brother, Jeremy, in Barry, Wales in 1968 and the home address was that of a boat, 'The

Gay Adventurer,' and that made sense as father had married a woman named 'Gay'. I had a half-brother! I was so elated and tearful!

It was at a real landmark in my life; I felt warm and triumphant; vindicated and powerful. Always cross the road and speak; never simply pass by; pause for a moment and speak from your heart. I'll never forget the moment when Jeremy's birth certificate arrived through the post; confirming everything I've told you.

Enter the dark ages; a twenty year hiatus before the 'Internet's' arrival. Enter a dull Local Education Officer trying to be interested. Enter Sylvie my eldest daughter, studying in the U.S.A. and the one who telephoned me one Sunday morning.

'Dad, you might want to sit down!'

Sitting down and somewhat puzzled I awaited the news she was about to relay.

'Dad, I think I have found your brother, Jeremy. He used to work at an ironmonger's shop called Johnson's Hardware on the island of St Lucia.'

'St Lucia! No wonder I couldn't find him!'

'But, get this Dad, he now works in Sittingbourne in a computer shop called 'Computers' Plus!'

St Lucia! St Lucia! That's why I could discover nothing about my father. He was thousands of miles away living in the Caribbean. Imagine that I had a likely half-brother living in the town where I was the local education officer; as they say, 'you couldn't make it up!'

On the Sunday evening I gathered my collection of birth, marriage and death certificates and excited beyond words, contacted my colleague Jayne to cancel all my appointments on Monday morning, because there was only one place I would be: outside 'Computer's Plus,' Sittingbourne.

I sent Jayne a first email on arrival outside 'Computer's Plus'

```
-----Original Message-----
From: Devreaux, John - CFE
Sent: 11 December 2006 10:13
To: Dartnell, Jayne - CFE
Subject: Meeting with fate?
```

Arrived at the Computer Plus place. Main shop empty- heart sank-

Small office operating upstairs so went in and asked if the bald guy behind the counter was Jeremy- no he's out and will be back in an hour- so I gave my first name and said I would return
I'm now sheltered and waiting away from the entrance- but watching and wondering-absolutely extraordinary.   John
----
Sent from my BlackBerry Wireless Handheld
```
-----Original Message-----
From: Dartnell, Jayne - CFE
Sent: 11 December 2006 10:23
To: Devreaux, John - CFE
Subject: RE: Meeting with fate?
Importance: High
```

What's his full name?

```
-----Original Message-----
From: Devreaux, John - CFE
Sent: 11 December 2006 10:30
To: Dartnell, Jayne - CFE
Subject: Re: Meeting with fate?
```

Jeremy Karl Robert Garner-Dobbs- he is 38 years old- born December 4th 1968 . My father who I have not heard anything about since the age of five will be 75 years old on December 14th this month

Phew-tension mounting- I am staying here until job's done- but of course it's an emotional roundabout- more for him- he probably doesn't know I even exist

```
John
-------------------------
Sent from my BlackBerry Wireless Handheld

-----Original Message-----
From: Devreaux, John - CFE
Sent: 11 December 2006 10:35
To: Dartnell, Jayne - CFE
Subject: Re: Meeting with fate?

The whole thing is totally unreal- I know. This guy went to
school in Castries- St Morne's and St Mary's
Both in St Lucia.

This major seismic breakthrough was brought about by daughter
Sylvie who was on line Googling in NY and found him.

He has done some work for Sittingbourne musicians- organising
their website. I know so much because Sylvie got into his
profile- but no pictures- so I don't know his face. John

-------------------------
Sent from my BlackBerry Wireless Handheld

-----Original Message-----
From: Dartnell, Jayne - CFE
To: Devreaux, John - CFE
Sent: 11 December 2006 10:37
Subject: RE: Meeting with fate?

Pretty bizarre.

Did you know that my brother Andrew's going to St Lucia next
year?

It would be funny if he's been trying to find you too.  Lovely
Xmas pressie if it all works out.  Good luck. x
```

I walked back into 'Computer's Plus' office and met the bald guy at the desk.

'I'm John,' I said, 'I'm the one who stopped by earlier, looking for Jeremy.'

'He's in his office....he's waiting for you.'

Carrying my briefcase full of documents which brought us together, I entered the room and Jeremy stood in front of me. We were of the same height and of similar build. We shook hands and hugged each other and he told me about my new sister and another new brother. He told me our father had died in 1998. I told him I had no photographs, nothing at all. He said he had photographs and not to worry.

I admired his thick black dreadlocks which brushed his shoulders and tears came when I saw a photograph of my biological father and I recognised him. That evening was also graced by my 'new' sister Elena who came to my house and filled it with great joy.

33.   The Cheesemonger

Off the rocky coast of western Ireland is the beautiful island of Caseus, rather circular like the moon but with a predominance of green rock. Today its provinces are ruled over by four royal chieftains: Brie the Great over Camembert, Gouda the Bountiful over Gruyere, Edam the Magnificent over Cheddari, and Roquefort the Fateful over Gorgonzola.

Sadly, all of these larger than life Chieftains had issues: Brie had cheesy braff, Gouda had cheesy feet, Edam told cheesy jokes, and Roquefort was always just cheesed off with life.

Brie the Great gassed villagers when he spoke; caused coughing and spitting among his courtiers and forced his wife to wear a snorkel and mask in bed, all due to his terrible braff. If you're wondering, Brie was nicknamed 'the Great' after he single handedly breathed on an invading force in Port Salut and saved his province of Camembert by toxic emissions, thereby gassing the lot. Brie was nicknamed 'the grate' because he just loved great grated cheese and wherever he had the opportunity he built blocks and blocks of cheese shaped high rise residences for his adoring people.

Chief Gouda was so different to Brie as he had the sweetest braff but the smelliest plates of meat you ever niffed. He wore his shoes indoors, in the bath, in the shower and even in the bed. Why? Obvious really; if he took his shoes off it caused the populace of Gruyere to fall over and choke on the odour of cheese. The song 'this little piggy went to market' was banned on pain of death and when his toenails were clipped, the doctor wore breathing equipment. He was called the 'bountiful' as he always donated his toenails to the poor and built many bridges based upon the shape of the arches of his beautiful but pongy feet.

Chieftain Edam was different again to the other three chieftains. He told cheesy jokes and always started by telling strangers that he was 'made' backwards. Ha! Ha! They'd go. Very funny, not!

Then he'd mix Edam with Eden and Edam with Madam and Edam with Adam and that led to a bible story. He was as mad as a cucumber in a shoe box.

 Edam was termed 'the magnificent' because of his beautiful palace in the middle of the yellow plains of Cheddari. 'Welcome to Cheddari' read the roadside sign,

EAT RESPONSIBLY!

DON'T GORGE ON CHEDDAR!

ENJOY YOUR STAY!

 Mayor Limburger

Last, but by no means least of these great Chieftains, was Roquefort the Fateful who ruled the hilly peninsula of Gorgonzola. Roquefort dined on macaroni cheese, Welsh rarebit, and cheese straws but to be brutally honest, he was never really happy or as he would say,

'We are cheesed orf,'

How was Roquefort deemed to be fateful? Well it all started when a few big cheeses from the Parliament decided that as Roquefort became 18 they would award him a title.

'From age 18?' he queried. 'Yes, from age 18.'

'But you have to do something special.'

' More special than inventing cheese and onion crisps?'

'Yes'

'More difficult than governing a province in which there are 246 kinds of cheese?'

'Yes'

'More challenging than making the word 'fate' from the cheesy word feta?'

'Yes'

.......and this is where I came in......the Cheesemonger......invited by Chieftain Roquefort the fateful to inspire the whole island with a new religious fervour , create Cathedral Cheddars in which the islanders can worship; summoned by a baby bell to call these lucky citizens to their devotions.

The Quarry

My sister Keira and I sneaked out of our cottage one rainy morning.
She turned to me and asked where we were going. I told her,"we
were gunna go up the woods cos I had a tip off."

 We dawdled along the track, passed the army camp, full of shouting
soldiers and big tanks practising their manoeuvres, ready to hunt our
enemies.

The soldiers created mock incidents like the time a vehicle appeared
to have crashed on the main street. There were pretend 'casualties'
swathed in bandages and daubed with fake blood but unfortunately
we were not privy to their little theatrical enactment.

For some time we stood watching in disbelief as the horrific
accident was acted out before us in all its gory glory. Eventually we
were told it was 'make believe' and a rehearsal in preparation for the
real thing. We would surely dream of that tonight!

We crossed the road and went into the wood at the edge of the field. It had been ploughed up quite a bit and was very muddy, and sticky on our feet. I could tell Keira didn't like the mud on her new shoes.

"I'll get told off," she said, and I knew she meant what she said, by the look in her eyes, and the way she just stood there, like one of the soldiers, anxious but defiant.

In the distance I could see the white cliffs of the chalk quarry and the gouged footprint made by the tracks of the tanks which had trundled through.Above us crows and jackdaws had made their nests up in the cracks and fissures of the cliffs, where they could best view life below. Someone at school had said that the cliffs were made from sea creatures that had died and lay down one on another like so many white stripes.

"John," said Keira, "what are we looking for?"

I was determined not to tell her yet.

"It's along here," I said to her,"somewhere near this edge...... I call it my discovery because I found it after the tip off, and I told the kids at school all about it."

"How much further?" she asked,"is it nearby?"

"Ah, can you see that young silver birch? It's near there....a bit further, Keira, just under the tree," I whispered. 'Ssssshh!'

And there it was in all its glory.....exactly where the tip off had said....its red top and white under fur all matted and splattered with mud and blood. Ah, dear beast lying there! How you have been dishonoured!

There it lay, in its final place at the edge of the field and at the edge of the pit.

"Did you bring me all this way to show me a dead fox?" Keira asked.

"What would you say if I cut off its brush? I could take it as a trophy to set alongside my Davy Crocket hat," I replied.

"Nah, that's disgusting!" she said, "leave it there, where it fell; there's nothing more we want from it and the farmer or soldier who shot it has had the last word. Yeah, let's leave it, poor thing, for the quarry."